Immortal Lite

Immortal Life

The Mukti Marg of Sri Jesus

Dhanjibhai Fakirbhai

B.R. Publishing Corporation
Delhi - 110 052

Published by:
B.R Publishing Corporation
425, Nimri Colony, Ashok Vihar, Phase-IV, Delhi-110 052
E-mail : brpc73@gmail.com

First Published 2020

© Pradip Ayer

ISBN 9789388789561

Cataloging in Publication Data--DK
Courtesy: D.K. Agencies (P) Ltd. <docinfo@dkagencies.com>

Fakirbhai, Dhanjibhai 1895-1967., author.
  [Sṛī hṛday gītā. Gujarati]
  Immortal life : the mukti marg of Sri Jesus / Dhanjibhai Fakirbhai.
    pages cm
  Translated from Gujarati.
  Previously published in 2014 as Song of the heart (Sri hriday gītā).
  Includes bibliographical references.
  ISBN 9789388789561

  1. Jesus Christ--Hindu interpretations. 2. Jesus Christ--Teachings. 3. Bhakti in literature. 4. Christianity and other religions--Hinduism. 5. Hinduism--Relations--Christianity. I. Title. II. Title: Song of the heart.

LCC BR128.H5F35 2020 | DDC 261.245   23

Contents

Chapter 1
Divya Darshan (The Divine Vision)

The seer said:
"Behind me, I heard a loud *vāni* (voice) that sounded like
the trumpet call of the army on the battleground.
I turned to look and saw seven golden *diyās* (lamps). 1

In the middle of the *diyās* I saw someone in human form. 2

He was wearing the robe of a holy man down to his ankles,
and he had a golden sash across his chest. 3

His eyes blazed like fire
and his feet were shining like refined bronze. 4

There were seven stars in his right hand;
his face shone like the full brightness of the sun. 5

His *sād* (voice) sounded like a mighty river. 6

When I saw him,
I fell prostrate at his feet as though dead. 7

Then he put his right hand on my head and said, 8

'Do not be afraid. I am the first and the last,
I am the beginning and the end.
I live forever. 9

What I open, no one can close.
What I close, no one can open.'" 10

Devadut *(messengers of God) sing his glory and praise:*
"Holy, Holy, Holy, *sarvashaktimān* (almighty) Lord God,
he who was, is, and is to come. 11

You alone are worthy to receive glory, honor, and power
because you have created everything.
By your will everything came into being. 12

You are the king of all the *yugs* (ages).
You alone are the eternal and invisible Lord. 13

You alone are eternal God, above all,
worthy to be praised at all times.
To you alone be honour and glory forever. 14

You alone are the *sampurn avatār* (complete incarnation)
of God invisible.

You are the light of God's glory and the exact *pratimā* (image) of God. 15

All of God's character is embodied in you.
In you, all of God's fullness dwells in *sharirarup* (bodily form)." 16

The seer said:
"God is revealed in *manushyarup* (human form),
and lived among us as a man. 17

He is filled with *kripā* (grace) and *satyatā* (truth).
His *kripā* is manifested
in the *sampurn avatār* (complete incarnation) of the Lord Jesus. 18

In him is life,
and his life is the light of mankind. 19

The light of Jesus shines in the darkness,
and, having come into the *duniyā* (world), enlightens everyone. 20

The darkness is receding,
and the real light is shining. 21

His *jivan* (life) was revealed and we saw him with our own eyes.
We were eye witnesses of the *prabhutā* (deity) of the Lord Jesus." 22

Spiritual knowledge named *Sri Hriday Gitā*;
here ends the first chapter named *Divya Darshan*.

Chapter 2
Uddhār (Redemption)

The Lord Jesus said:
"I have come to heal the brokenhearted,
to release those in prison,
and to give sight to the blind. 1

I have come into the *jagat* (world) not to judge,
but that through me the *jagat* may have *uddhār* (redemption). 2

I have come for *uddhār* of the *jagat*
rather than to judge the *jagat*. 3

Oh, those who labour and are laid under a heavy weight,
all of you come to me and I will give you rest. 4

The one who comes to me I will not cast out." 5

Many rejects and adharmo *(unrighteous people) were following the Lord Jesus.* 6

At that time the Lord Jesus said:
"Those who are healthy do not need a doctor,
but those who are sick need a doctor. 7

It is not the *dhārmik* (righteous) but *pāpi* (sinners)
I have come to invite." 8

Jesus went to a rejected person's house.
At that time Jesus said: 9

"I have come to search out and save those who are lost. 10

It is not my desire that even one of these little ones be destroyed. 11

If a *pāpi* (sinner) sincerely repents
there is *ānand* (joy) in heaven." 12

People brought a person who had polio to the Lord Jesus.
Seeing their shraddhā (faith) *at that time he said to the man,* 13

"Child, take courage, you are given *māfi* (forgiveness) for your *pāp* (sins).
Arise, pick up your cot and go home." 14

That man immediately got up
and went to his own home praising God. 15

A fallen woman from the city came to the Lord Jesus,
and began to wash his feet with her tears. 16

The Lord Jesus said to her:
"You are given *māfi* (forgiveness) for your *pāp* (sins).
Your *vishwās* (faith) has saved you, go home in *shānti* (peace)." 17

A person with leprosy fell at Jesus' feet and said,
"Lord, if it may be your will, then you are able to cleanse me." 18

The Lord felt compassion, touched him with his hand, and said,
"I am willing, be clean." 19

He immediately recovered from his leprosy,
and was cleansed. 20

Having been given a death sentence on a cross,
 a convicted thief said to the Lord Jesus,
"Lord, remember me in your heavenly kingdom." 21

The Lord answered him:
"I assuredly say to you that
today you will be with me where heavenly people dwell." 22

A bhakt *(devotee) said:*
"I am indebted to the Lord
because he counted me *vishwāsu* (faithful),
admitting me into his *sevā* (service). 23

I used abusive language, and I was a harasser and oppressor.
Nevertheless, I was shown *dayā* (mercy). 24

The *kripā* (grace) of our Lord was so abundant
that my *vishwās* (faith) and *prem* (love) for God
were born within me. 25

This saying is *vishwāsniya* (faithful)
and perfectly worthy to be accepted.
The Lord Jesus came into this *jagat* (world) to save *pāpi* (sinners);
I am the chief of them." 26

Spiritual knowledge named *Sri Hriday Gitā*;
here ends the second chapter named *Uddhār*.

Chapter 3
Shraddhāyog (The Yoga of Faith)

A shraddhāvān *(believer) said*:
"Without *shraddhā* (faith),
it is not possible to please the Lord." 1

The Lord said:
"My *bhakt* (devotee) will live by *vishwās* (faith)." 2

Two blind men came to Jesus and said,
"Lord, have *dayā* (mercy) on us." 3

The Lord asked:
"What do you want me to do for you?" 4

They said:
"Lord, open our eyes." 5

The Lord said to them:
"Do you have *vishwās* (faith) that I am able to do this?" 6

The blind ones said:
"Yes, Lord." 7

At that time the Lord, moved with dayā *(mercy),*
touched their eyes and said,
"Let it happen to you according to your *vishwās*." 8

Immediately they could see, and they followed Jesus. 9

The Lord said:
"Those who do not see, will see.
This is why I have come into the *jagat* (world). 10

The one who is walking in the darkness
does not know where he is going. 11

I am the light of the *jagat*.
The one who follows me will not walk in darkness,
but will receive the illumination of life. 12

Anyone who has *vishwās* (faith) in me will not stay in darkness.
This is why I have come as *prakāshrup* (light). 13

As long as you have light,
have *vishwās* in that light,
so that you become a child of the light." 14

A woman with a hemorrhage for twelve years
had endured much from doctors.
No one had been able to heal her. 15

She came up behind the Lord and touched the hem of his clothes
because she reasoned in her own mind that
"if I can only touch the Lord's clothes, then I will be healed."
She did so and her bleeding stopped immediately. 16

The Lord turned, saw her, and said,
"Daughter, take courage, your *shraddhā* (faith) has healed you.
Go in *shānti* (peace)." 17

A leader of the community came to the Lord and humbly said,
"Lord, I am not worthy for you to come under my roof,
but if you just say the word then my servant will be healed." 18

The Lord said to the community leader,
"Be it done according to your *vishwās* (faith)."
At that exact hour, his servant was healed. 19

A shishya *(disciple) said,*
"The Lord reveals that which is not as if it is.
Where there is no place for hope,
we keep believing with hope. 20

The word which he gave he is powerful to fulfill.
Having kept trust in such fulfillment, stay firm in *vishwās*." 21

Shishyas *(disciples) implored the Lord Jesus*:
"Lord, increase our *vishwās*." 22

The Lord Jesus answered:
"I decisively say to you that
if you have *vishwās* like a mustard seed,
then nothing will be impossible to you. 23

Ask and it will be given to you,
but ask with *vishwās* and without doubting. 24

The one who doubts is like a wave of
the sea, blown and tossed by the wind.
A double-minded person is unstable in everything he does. 25

To those who have *vishwās*, all things are possible.
Do not doubt in your *man* (heart). 26

If anyone does not doubt in his own *man*
but has *vishwās* that what I say will happen,
it will happen for him. 27

Through the testing of your *vishwās*, patience is created." 28

A shraddhāvān *(believer) said*:
"The Lord is *vishwāsniya* (faithful).
He will not allow a test to be upon us
that is over and above our *shakti* (strength)." 29

People asked the Lord Jesus:
"What should we do to do the works of God?" 30

The Lord Jesus answered:
"Have *vishwās* in me, this alone is the work of God. 31

You have not heard the *vāni* (voice) of God,
and you have not seen his *swarup* (form). 32

The one who sees me, sees God.
The one who has *vishwās* in me, has *vishwās* in God. 33

The one who has *vishwās* on me will not die,
but he will obtain *ananta jivan* (everlasting life). 34

I give *shāswat jivan* (eternal life) to you,
and no one will pluck you from my hand. 35

17

The one who hears my word and has *vishwās*
will not be condemned, but having departed from death,
will come into *amaratva* (immortality). 36

The one who has *vishwās* in me will not remain in darkness,
for I have come into the *jagat* (world) as a light. 37

The one who has *vishwās* in me is not condemned,
but the one who does not have *vishwās* in me is already condemned
because light came into the *jagat*.
Nevertheless, he preferred darkness more than light. 38

I am giving my *shānti* (peace) to you.
Do not allow your *hriday* (heart) to be troubled
nor give in to fear.
You should have *vishwās* in me. 39

Place your worries upon me
because I care for you.
Do not worry about anything, but bring your requests to me. 40

I know what is important to you before you inquire. 41

Look at the birds of the air;
I attend to them. 42

Consider the bushes of wild flowers;
I dress them.
All of the hairs on your head are counted. 43

So, do not fear;
not one hair on your head will be destroyed." 44

The shraddhāvān *(believers) said*:
"Not in ourselves,
but we trust in the Lord. 45

I know the one whom I have trusted.
The one who has given me the promise
is *vishwāsyogya* (trustworthy). 46

From his own glorious and plentiful store of wealth,
the Lord will fully satisfy all of our needs." 47

The Lord said:
"Do not look at visible things;
focus on the things which are invisible. 48

Visible things are momentary;
but invisible things are eternal. 49

Vishwās (faith) is the assurance of that which is hoped for
and the proof of invisible things. 50

Stay unwavering through *vishwās* as if seeing invisible things." 51

The shraddhāvān *(believers) said,*
"We walk by *shraddhā* (faith) and not by sight.
We focus on the Lord Jesus,
the captain of our *vishwās* and perfecter of our *shraddhā*. 52

Let us hold firm until the end the trust that we had in the beginning.
Let us increase in our *param pavitra vishwās* (eternal holy faith). 53

Our *vishwās* should not depend on human *jñān* (wisdom),
but on the power of God. 54

Lord, fill us with *akhand harsh* (complete gladness) and *shānti* (peace) as we keep the *vishwās*." 55

Spiritual knowledge named *Sri Hriday Gitā*;
here ends the third chapter named *Shraddhāyog*.

Chapter 4
Bhaktiyog (The Yoga of Devotion)

The Lord Jesus said:
"The ones who worship me
should do my *bhajan* (worship)
with *ātmā* (spirit) and *satya* (truth/reality).
I desire such *bhakts* (devotees)." 1

A bhakt *said:*
"Let us do his *sevā* (service) respectfully.
In this way the Lord will be pleased." 2

The Lord Jesus said:
"Love me with your entire *hriday* (heart), entire life,
entire *buddhi* (intellect), and entire strength. 3

The one who loves me, I will love
and I will reveal myself to him. 4

Make your *hriday shuddh* (pure) in order to praise me.
Blessed is he who is *shuddh* in *man* (heart);
he will receive my *darshan* (vision). 5

My *dās* (servants) will worship me,
and they will behold my face. 6

My *bhakts* (devotees) hear my *sād* (voice),
and they follow me. 7

I know the ones who are my own,
and my own recognize me." 8

The shishyas *(disciples) said:*
"As beloved children, let us become the ones who imitate the Lord,
understanding what the will of the Lord is
and what is acceptable to the Lord." 9

The Lord said:
"I am your Lord and *swāmi* (master).
I only am your guru,
and you are all brothers." 10

The shishyas *(disciples) said:*
"My Lord and my God!"
They fell at his feet and worshipped him. 11

They entreated the Lord,
"Lord, teach us to pray."

The Lord said:
"Do not babble meaninglessly while praying.
When you pray, enter your room, shut your door,
and pray to the Lord secretly. 12

Come near me and you will receive rest in your daily life.
Pray in your *ātmā* (spirit) at all times with all types of prayers
and entreat thankfully, praising the Lord in every circumstance. 13

Always pray and do not become lazy.
Keep praying. Do the Lord's *sevā* (service).
Remain committed to *bhakti* (devotion) with perseverance." 14

A bhakt *said:*
"Let us come near
to the Lord with *shuddh* (pure) *hriday* (hearts)
and complete resolve,
having kept *shraddhā* (faith). 15

Let us go near the Lord's *kripāsan* (gracious throne) with
the courage to receive *dayā* (mercy) and to obtain *kripā* (grace)
for assistance in critical situations. 16

We enter the Lord's presence with courage and trust
through *vishwās* (faith) in the Lord. 17

We do not know what to appropriately pray for.
However, the *ātmā* (spirit) of the Lord himself intercedes for us,
helping us in our weaknesses.
We are the *sevaks* (servants) of the Lord
through the *ātmā* of the Lord." 18

The Lord Jesus said:
"If you stay in me and my words remain in you,
then you should ask for whatever you desire
and you will receive it. 19

Whatever you ask for with *shraddhā* (faith) in prayer
you will receive. 20

You will receive all that you ask for in prayer
if you pray believing that you have received it. 21

Ask and you will receive
so your *ānand* (joy) will become full.
Let my *ānand* remain in you,
and let your *ānand* become full. 22

Be joyful, always be joyful in the Lord
through songs, through praises,
and through *ādhyātmik* (spiritual) songs.
In your *hriday* (heart), sing songs and
bhajans (spiritual songs) to the Lord. 23

Your *man* (heart) will receive *ānand*,
and no one can take your *ānand* from you." 24

A bhakt *said:*
"We are rejoicing with fullness of *ānand* before the Lord." 25

When the Lord sat at dinner a woman applied
a pound of priceless perfume on his feet, 26

and she wiped his feet clean with her long braid of hair.
The fragrance of the perfume spread throughout the entire house. 27

At that time the Lord said,
"This lady has done what she was able to do. 28

Worship your Lord
and do his *sevā* (service) alone. 29

29

With single-minded focus, do the *sevā* of the Lord.
Contentment together with *bhakti* (devotion) is greatly profitable. 30

No one is able to serve two masters.
You are not able to do the *sevā* of God and seek material wealth. 31

Whenever you pray,
give *māfi* (forgiveness) to anyone
if they have done anything against you. 32

As the Lord has given you *kshāmā* (forgiveness),
you give *kshāmā* to one another.
As beloved children follow my example. 33

When you pray, at that time say:
'Oh Lord, give *māfi* for our offences
just as we ourselves also give *māfi* to our offenders.' 34

I give you my *shānti* (peace).
Be at *shānti*. 35

My *shānti*, which is beyond all understanding,
will safeguard your *hriday* (hearts) and *man* (minds)." 36

The shraddhāvān *(believers) said:*
"The *swāmi* (master) of *shānti* will stay with us. 37

Let us keep ourselves established in the love of God,
increasing in *param pavitra vishwās* (supreme holy faith)
and praying in the *pavitra ātmā* (Holy Spirit)." 38

Spiritual knowledge named *Sri Hriday Gitā*;
here ends the fourth chapter named *Bhaktiyog*.

Chapter 5
Ātmā ane Paramātmāyog
(The Yoga of Spirit and Supreme Spirit)

The Lord Jesus said:
"I will come to stay with you always. 1

I am standing in front of the door
of your *hriday* (heart) and knocking.
If anyone, hearing my *vāni* (voice), opens the door,
then I will come in and stay with him. 2

If anyone loves me he will keep my word.
Then I will come near him and dwell with him. 3

The one who obeys my commands
dwells in me and I dwell in him. 4

God is love. Therefore the one who dwells in love
dwells in God, and God dwells in him." 5

A bhakt *said:*
"Through *vishwās* (faith) the Lord dwells in our *hriday* (hearts)." 6

The Lord Jesus said:
"You live in me and I will live in you. 7

If anyone does not live in me,
he is thrown out like a branch and withers." 8

A bhakt *said:*
"If anyone obeys the word of God,
in him the love of God is truly made complete.
In this way we know that we are in God. 9

The one who says 'I live in him' must
walk as the Lord walked." 10

The Lord Jesus said:
"The one who has me has life,
the one who does not have me does not have life;
I am living so you also will live." 11

A bhakt *said:*
"The life which I have in the body
is only by *vishwās* (faith) in the Lord. 12

The Lord is increasing and I am decreasing; this is necessary. 13

I am living, nevertheless now it is not me,
but the Lord living in me. 14

For me to live is Christ; the Lord Jesus is my life. 15

The Lord was pleased to reveal himself in me. 16

The one who is joined to the Lord
becomes one *ātmā* (spirit) with the Lord. 17

I also desire to receive the Lord Christ,
and become *ekrup* (one) with him. 18

We are all being transformed,
beholding the glory of the Lord in a mirror with an open face.
From the *ātmā* (spirit) of the Lord we are taking on
the *swarup* (image) of the Lord with ever increasing glory." 19

The Lord said:
"The fruits which I produce within are these:
love, joy, peace, patience, kindness, goodness,
faithfulness, humility, and self-control." 20

A bhakt said:
"We are the Lord's *mandir* (temple),
and the Lord's *ātmā* (spirit) dwells in us. 21

The *mandir* of the Lord is *pavitra* (holy),
and we are that *mandir*. 22

The *ātmā* of the Lord is in us;
our body is his *mandir*.
Let us give the Lord glory through our bodies. 23

The body is for the Lord,
and the Lord is for the body. 24

The *ātmā* of the Lord helps us in our weaknesses." 25

The Lord Jesus said:
"Do not worry about 'what will we say or how will we say it.'
For what to say at that moment will be given to you. 26

Because what you are speaking is not from you,
but in you my *ātmā* is speaking. 27

The *ātmā* of *satya* (truth/reality) will guide you into all *satya*." 28

Spiritual knowledge named *Sri Hriday Gitā*;
here ends the fifth chapter named *Ātmā ane Paramātmāyog*.

Chapter 6
Premyog (The Yoga of Love)

The Lord Jesus said:
"I have loved you.
Live in my love." 1

A bhakt *said:*
"We know the love of God is directed toward us,
and we have believed in his love. 2

We love because the Lord first loved us." 3

The Lord Jesus said:
"If you love me, then you will keep my commands.
If you keep my commands, then you will live in my love.
My love lives in you, and I live in you. 4

Love one another in the same way as I loved you.
Walk in the love with which I have loved you." 5

A bhakt *said:*
"God loved the *duniyā* (world),
and came to the *jagat* (world). 6

Because the Lord Jesus Christ gave his own life on our behalf,
we also should give our lives for our brothers. 7

If the Lord so loved us,
we also ought to love one another. 8

The love of the Lord Jesus compels us." 9

The Lord said:
"The one who does not love, does not recognize God
because God is love. 10

39

The one who loves God
ought to love his own brothers. 11

The one who loves the birth-giver
also loves the one who is born of him." 12

A bhakt *said:*
"From the *ātmā* (Spirit) of the Lord dwelling within us,
the love of the Lord has begun flowing
within our *antahkaran* (inner being). 13

If we love one another,
the Lord lives in us
and his love has become complete in us. 14

By remaining obedient to *satya* (truth/reality)
and for the sake of genuine love for the brothers,
we have made our *man* (hearts) *pavitra* (holy). 15

So let us love one another from our *antahkaran* and with sincerity
because love covers a heap of *pāp* (sins). 16

Let us love in conduct and *satya*. 17

Whoever has the material wealth of this *jagat* (world)
and sees his own brother in need
yet is not compassionate towards him;
how is the love of God within him? 18

Love does nothing evil to his own neighbour,
therefore love is perfect obedience of the *niyam* (law)." 19

The Lord Jesus said:
"Take up that love which is the bond of *sampurnatā* (perfection).
Whatever you do, do it from love. 20

Love one another as you love yourself;
love each other deeply. 21

Perform *sevā* (service) towards one another with love.
Lift one another's heavy loads. 22

Love from a *shuddh* (pure) *hriday* (heart),
a good *antahkaran* (conscience),
and *shraddhā* (faith) without pretence. 23

Love your enemies and do good to them.
Make an effort to enrich one another, and all mankind. 24

Love is tolerant and benevolent.
Love does not act jealously, does not boast, is not swelled with pride,
and does not behave in an unworthy manner. 25

Love does not celebrate injustice,
but celebrates *satya* (truth/reality). 26

Love puts up with all things, endures all things,
believes all things as true, and hopes all things.
Love never runs out." 27

Hearing that, a bhakt *said:*
"May the Lord make our love increase
towards one another and towards all mankind. 28

For those who love the Lord,
in the end everything turns out beneficially." 29

The Lord said:
"There is no fear in love.
The one who fears has not been perfected in love.
Perfect love banishes fear." 30

Having become full of ānand *(joy), a* bhakt *said:*
"Who will be able to separate us from
the love of the Lord Jesus Christ;
trouble, hardship, persecution, famine, danger, sword? 31

No one is able to separate us from the love of the Lord Jesus Christ.
Keep yourself firm in the love of the Lord." 32

The Lord said:
"Putting your roots and foundation in love,
understand the breadth, length, height, and depth of my love
which is beyond the understanding of humankind." 33

Spiritual knowledge named *Sri Hriday Gitā*;
here ends the sixth chapter named *Premyog*.

Chapter 7
Karmyog (The Yoga of Works)

The Lord said:
"The ones who keep *shraddhā* (faith) in me
become concerned with doing good deeds. 1

As the body without *ātmā* (spirit) is lifeless,
so *shraddhā* without good deeds is also lifeless. 2

Through virtuous deeds *vishwās* (faith) is made perfect.
Only the *vishwās* which produces good deeds
through love is beneficial." 3

In answer, a bhakt *said:*
"We are the Lord's handiwork.
We were created to do *satkarm* (good works). 4

My food is to fulfill the will of the Lord
and to complete his work." 5

The Lord Jesus said:
"As a good manager you should use whatever *dān* (gift)
you have received from God
for doing *sevā* (service) to one another." 6

On this, a bhakt *said:*
"Every perfect and complete *dān* is from above,
and descends from our father, God. 7

People are not able to get anything
unless it is given to them by God. 8

The one to whom much is entrusted,
from him much is required.
The one who is *vishwāsu* (faithful) in a little
is also *vishwāsu* in much. 9

Be ready to do every good work.
Do not be unproductive; be zealous in *ātmā* (spirit)." 10

The Lord Jesus said:
"Do the *sevā* (service) of the Lord.
Every branch in me which bears no fruit is cut away.
Every branch which bears fruit is cleansed to produce more fruit." 11

The one who has *vishwās* (faith) in me
will also do the work which I am doing,
and will do more works than that. 12

As a branch by itself cannot bear fruit without being in the vine,
so you cannot bear fruit without being in me. 13

The one who lives in me and in whom I dwell will bear much fruit.
You cannot do anything if you live separate from me." 14

A bhakt *said:*
"We are not worthy of doing anything from ourselves,
but our sufficiency is from the Lord. 15

He has made us worthy to become *sevaks* (servants) of the *ātmā* (Spirit).
We are the ones who do *sevā* from the *ātmā* of the Lord,
and we do not trust in ourselves. 16

The Lord is the one who inspires us to desire and to achieve
according to his own pleasure. 17

I cannot do anything of my own accord.
The Lord does his own work by dwelling within me. 18

I am laboring according to his inspiration
which strongly inspires me.
It is not me, but his *kripā* (grace) which is in me. 19

As the Lord gives me strength,
I am able to do all things with his help." 20

The Lord said:
"My strength becomes perfect in weakness." 21

A bhakt *said:*
"The strength of the Lord rests upon me.
So that when I am weak I am strong. 22

The Lord is able to do far more for us than we can ask or imagine
according to his strength which is working within us. 23

Let us realize the importance of his *shakti* (power)
in us who have *vishwās* (faith),
according to the strength of his *mahān shakti* (great power)." 24

The Lord said:
"After having obeyed all the commands which were given to you,
you should say that we are worthless *chākar* (servants).
We have only done what was our duty." 25

On that, a bhakt *said:*
"The one who has entered the rest of the Lord
has taken rest from his own work. 26

We who have *vishwās* (faith) are entering rest. 27

Whatever we do, let us do it from a sincere *dil* (heart),
understanding that what we are doing
is not for people but for the Lord. 28

We are doing the *sevā* (service) of the Lord Jesus.
In word or deed, let us do everything in the name of the Lord Jesus. 29

Whether we eat or drink or whatever we do,
let us do it all for the sake of the glory of the Lord." 30

The Lord said:
"Keep doing good deeds and continue to increase
in every good work. 31

Fulfill the will of God in your life as my *dās* (servants),
not as people-pleasers but from a sincere *hriday* (heart). 32

Always remain engrossed in the work of your Lord
because your work in the Lord is not meaningless. 33

If anyone offers a cup of cold water in my name
he will not lose his reward. 34

If anyone welcomes a small child in my name he welcomes me. 35

When I was hungry you fed me.
When I was thirsty you made me drink. 36

When I was naked you dressed me.
When I was an outsider you kept me as your guest. 37

When I was sick you visited me.
When I was in prison you inquired after me. 38

Whatever you did for just one of these insignificant brothers of mine,
you also did it for me." 39

At that time a bhakt *said:*
"Christ Jesus is Lord and we are everyone's *sevaks* (servants)
for the Lord's sake. 40

Let those who live not live for the sake of themselves,
but live for the Lord's sake. 41

May the glory of the Lord increase through my body,
whether by life or death, 42

because for me to live is the Lord Jesus Christ
and to die is gain." 43

Spiritual knowledge named *Sri Hriday Gitā*;
here ends the seventh chapter named *Karmyog*.

Chapter 8
Rājyog (The Yoga of the Kingdom)

The Lord Jesus said:
"May your heavenly kingdom be established
on earth as it is in heaven. 1

The time is now fulfilled;
the heavenly kingdom is near.
Do *paschyātāp* (repentance) and keep *shraddhā* (faith) in me." 2

People asked:
 "When will the kingdom of God come?"
The Lord answered:
"The kingdom of God does not come in a visible way. 3

It will not be said, 'Look! It is here or it is there,' 4

because the kingdom of God is among you.
The kingdom of God is within you." 5

The Lord called a child to come
and stand among the *shishyas* (disciples). 6

And the Lord said:
"If you do not change and become like a child,
then you will not be able to enter the heavenly kingdom. 7

The one who does not receive the heavenly kingdom as a child
will not be able to enter it. 8

Whoever humbles himself as a child
is greatest of all in the heavenly kingdom. 9

Blessed are those who are humble in *ātmā* (spirit)
because the heavenly kingdom is theirs. 10

The heavenly kingdom is
righteous living, *shānti* (peace), and *ānand* (joy)
through the *pavitra ātmā* (Holy Spirit). 11

You must first search for the heavenly kingdom
and its righteousness,
then everything else will be given to you. 12

The heavenly kingdom is like this:
a man plants a seed in soil.
He sleeps at night and stands guard during the day.
The seed sprouts and grows,
but how this happens the man does not know. 13

Soil bears fruit of its own accord.
First a sprout, after that the stalk of the plant,
and after that ripe grain in the stalk. 14

The impure, wicked, and those enticed by money
have no place in the kingdom of God. 15

It is easier for a camel to go through the eye of a needle
than for the rich to enter the heavenly kingdom. 16

The heavenly kingdom is like a merchant
searching for a fine pearl. 17

When that merchant discovered a priceless pearl
he sold everything he had and bought that pearl. 18

Those who are referred to as 'ruler'
exercise mastery over people.
Those who are powerful
exercise authority over people,
but it is not so among us. 19

If anyone wants to become first,
then let him become last of all and *sevak* (servant) of all. 20

I am a king, but my kingdom is not of this *sansār* (world). 21

Those who desire to gain a higher status,
let them become *sevaks* of all.
The one who desires to be first,
let him become *sevak* of all. 22

As I did not come to receive *sevā* (service) but to do *sevā*,
you act in the same way." 23

The *shishyas* (disciples) sat to eat,
and at that time the Lord Jesus himself rose from the meal.
He removed his own outer garment,
took a towel, and tied it around his waist. 24

Then having poured water into a vessel,
he washed the *shishyas'* feet.
With the towel he wore he began to dry their feet. 25

After this the Lord said:
"If I the Lord and guru have washed your feet,
then you should wash one another's feet. 26

As I have done to you,
in the same way you should do also,
for I have given you an example. 27

Among you one who is great must become lowly,
and he who is a leader
must become one who does *sevā* (service). 28

I am among you as a doer of *sevā*.
So all of you embrace humility to do *sevā* to each other. 29

Everyone, from a humble attitude,
count each other better than yourself.
You should determine to give respect to others
more than to yourself. 30

I have resolved to give you the kingdom.
You are the people of the heavenly kingdom.
You are a chosen *jāti* (people),
a *pavitra prajā* (holy people)
and the *khās lok* (special people) of the Lord. 31

The one who merely says 'Lord, Lord' to me
will not enter the heavenly kingdom,
but only the one who acts according to my will may enter. 32

We must enter the heavenly kingdom
having experienced many difficulties.
The ones who endure pain for the kingdom of God
should count themselves worthy to enter the kingdom. 33

Blessed are those who are persecuted because
of being solely devoted to *dharm* (God's righteous ways),
because the heavenly kingdom is theirs. 34

Love your enemies;
pray for those who plot against you. 35

Do good to those who act with malice towards you.
Bless those who give you *shrāp* (curse). 36

Pray for those who disrespect you.
In this way you become children of the heavenly father, 37

because he causes his sun to rise on the evil and the good
and he causes rain to pour down on the *dhārmik* (righteous)
and the *adhārmik* (unrighteous). 38

The heavenly father shows *dayā* (mercy)
so you should show *dayā* as well. 39

Do not fight with evil people.
If anyone slaps your cheek,
then you should also offer the other cheek. 40

If someone demands to take your shirt,
then give him your coat also. 41

Give to anyone who asks something of you.
If someone wants to borrow what you have,
do not refuse him. 42

Whoever has two coats,
give one to the person who does not have one.
The one who has food, do the same. 43

In the way that you want people to treat you,
treat them in the same way. 44

Do not slander anyone;
be sure to act towards all people
with complete humility. 45

Rejoice with those who celebrate.
Cry with those who cry. 46

Do not render people injustice,
and they will not render injustice to you.
Do not condemn anyone,
and no one will condemn you.
Give *kshamā* (forgiveness),
and *ksamā* will be granted to you as well. 47

If your brother acts wrongly against you seven times in one day,
and seven times says 'I repent,'
then give him *māfi* (forgiveness). 48

If you do not give *māfi* for people's *aprādh* (wrongdoings)
from your *dil* (heart),
then your *aprādh* will also not be given *māfi*. 49

They who grasp the sword
will be destroyed by the sword. 50

Blessed are the ones who give good counsel;
they are called children of God. 51

Blessed are those who are humble;
they will inherit the earth." 52

After they heard all this, the shishyas (*disciples) shouted out:*
"To the Lord on high, glory;
on earth, *shānti* (peace), and best wishes to mankind." 53

Spiritual knowledge named *Sri Hriday Gitā*;
here ends the eighth chapter named *Rājyog*.

Chapter 9
Prākritik ane Ādhyātmik
(The Natural and the Spiritual)

The Lord said:
"A good tree cannot give rotten fruit.
A bad tree cannot give good fruit. 1

A good man brings out good things
from the storehouse of his *man* (heart).
An evil man brings out evil things from an evil storehouse. 2

Out of the *hriday* (heart) come evil thoughts, murder, adultery,
theft, false witness and slander; these defile people. 3

You appear *nyāyi* (righteous) in front of people,
but God knows what is in your *antahkaran* (inner being). 4

You clean the outside of the plate and cup,
but your *antar* (inside) is filled with injustice and evil. 5

Give your inner self as *dāndharm* (offering),
and behold, everything to you is *shuddh* (pure)! 6

What a man plants is what he reaps.
Whatever he plants in respect to his body will reap him destruction.
What he plants in respect to his *ātmā* (spirit),
he will reap from the *ātmā*; *shāswat jivan* (eternal life). 7

Bodily nature is animosity with God;
bodily nature is death.
Spiritual nature is *jivan* (life) and *shānti* (peace). 8

The body is in opposition to the *ātmā*
and the *ātmā* is in opposition to the body
because they are mutually in opposition." 9

A shishya (*disciple*) *heard this and said:*
"I know that there is not one good thing in my body
because the good which I desire is what I do not do,
but the evil which I do not desire I continually do. 10

I see a different *niyam* (law) in the members of the body
which fights against the *niyam* of the *man* (mind)
and which brings the members of the body
into bondage under the *niyam* of *pāp* (sin). 11

I am so very unfortunate!
Who will release me from this body of death?" 12

The Lord Jesus said:
"That which is born from body is body.
That which is born from *ātmā* (spirit) is *ātmā*. 13

I definitely say that
if any man has not received a new birth,
then he is not able to see the kingdom of God. 14

If anyone has not been born of *ātmā*,
then he is not able to enter the kingdom of God. 15

Whoever accepts me,
or, in other words, whoever has *vishwās* (faith) in my name,
to them I give authority to become sons of God. 16

They are not born of the desire of the body
nor of human desire, but of God. 17

Not born from destructible seed, but from indestructible;
they have been given *punarjanma* (rebirth)." 18

At that time, from boundless harsh *(gladness), a* bhakt *said:*
"The *ātmā* (spirit) of the Lord gives witness to our *ātmā*
that we are the children of God.
We have received the *ātmā* of adoption
from which we cry out, 'Lord, Father.' 19

We have been given *punarjanma* (rebirth) to an
imperishable, pure, and unfading inheritance." 20

The Lord said:
"Whoever are led by my *ātmā* (spirit) are the sons of God.
Walk through the *ātmā*, and, in so doing,
you will not gratify the *vāsanā* (lusts) of the body." 21

A bhakt *said:*
"The body with its *vāsanā* is an abode of death,
but the *ātmā* is alive because the Lord resides in us. 22

The *ātmā* of the Lord resides in us,
therefore we are not of body, but we are *ādhyātmik* (spiritual).
We walk not according to the body, but according to the *ātmā*. 23

The *niyam* (law) of the *ātmā* of the life of the Lord
has released me from the *niyam* of *pāp* (sin) and death." 24

At that time, the Lord said:
"The one who is born of God does not commit *pāp*
because the seed of God resides in him. 25

He is not able to commit *pāp*
because he has been born of God. 26

He has put away the old humanity with its practices,
and has put on a new humanity
which is being renewed
according to the *pratimā* (image) of his creator. 27

He has been completely transformed
by the renewal of his *man* (mind)
together with the newness of his *hriday* (heart). 28

Be focused on things above,
not on things of the earth." 29

The shishyas *(disciples) said:*
"That which is old has been done away with.
Behold, it has become new!" 30

Spiritual knowledge named *Sri Hriday Gitā*;
here ends the ninth chapter named *Prākritik ane Ādhyātmik*.

Chapter 10
Mukti (Salvation)

The Lord Jesus said:
"For this alone I was born,
and for this alone I came into the *jagat* (world),
so that I may bear witness about *satya* (truth/reality). 1

I am *satya*.
Everyone who is of *satya* listens to my *vāni* (voice). 2

You will know *satya*,
and *satya* will give you *mukti* (freedom/salvation)." 3

Some people said:
"We have never come into the servitude of anyone,
so, why are you saying 'you will get *mukti*'?" 4

The Lord Jesus answered:
"The desires that dwell in people make them their *dās* (slave). 5

The one who continues to commit *pāp* (sin) is a *dās* of *pāp*.
You are enslaved to the one you surrender to in obedience,
but if I give you *mukti*, then you will have genuine *mukti*. 6

Breaking the law is *pāp*; all injustice is *pāp*.
The one who knows to do well but does not do so,
to him that is *pāp*.
All that is not from *vishwās* (faith) is *pāp*. 7

Every man, having been led away and enticed
by his own *durvāsanā* (evil lusts) falls into strong temptation. 8

74

After *durvāsanā* has conceived, it gives birth to *pāp*.
Pāp, becoming fully matured, gives birth to death. 9

I am the one who gives *mukti* to people from their *pāp*. 10

I cause people to repent in their *man* (hearts),
and I give them *kshamā* (forgiveness) for their *pāp*
so that afterwards they may not remain in slavery to *pāp*." 11

A bhakt *said:*
"In the Lord we have *uddhār* (redemption),
which is *kshamā* for *pāp*.
The Lord Jesus has set us free from the kingdom of darkness,
and has brought us into his own kingdom. 12

The children are of flesh and blood,
so likewise the Lord Jesus also joined in with them. 13

Therefore, by himself conquering death,
 he brings *mukti* (freedom/salvation) to those
who have been eternally enslaved by the fear of death." 14

The Lord Jesus said:
"I give them *ananta jivan* (eternal life)
and they will never be destroyed.
No one will forcefully snatch them from my hand." 15

A bhakt *said:*
"The Lord Jesus has freed us out of this evil *sansār* (world). 16

We become partakers of the nature of God,
having been given *mukti* (freedom/salvation)
from the wickedness
caused by *sansāri* (worldly) *durvāsanā* (evil lusts). 17

The Lord is *ātmā* (spirit),
and where the *ātmā* of the Lord is
there is also *swatantratā* (freedom). 18

The Lord has given us *swatantratā* for *swatantratā*.
Let us remain strong
and never again come beneath the yoke of servitude. 19

Having been released from *pāp*,
and, having become the *dās* (servants) of the Lord,
we are becoming *pavitra* (holy) and as a result receive *ananta jivan* (eternal life)." 20

The Lord said:
"From now on, you are not *dās* (servants) but sons,
⸳nd if you are sons, then you are also heirs." 21

A bhakt *said:*
"The Lord has delivered us so that
we may be counted as his sons." 22

Again, the Lord said to the shishyas *(disciples):*
"You are beloved to me.
I chose you from the beginning for *moksh* (salvation)
through the *vishuddhi* (purity) of the *ātmā* (spirit)
and through *shraddhā* (faith) in *satya* (truth/reality). 23

I have appointed you to follow me and stay with me. 24

I have determined that my *pratimā* (image) will be created in you. 25

I will bring you to myself
so that where I am, there you will also be." 26

A person asked:
"Lord, are the ones who receive *mukti* (salvation) just a few?" 27

The Lord Jesus answered:
"Strive to enter by the narrow door
because many will seek to enter but will not be able to enter. 28

The way leading to destruction is wide and the door is wide as well.
Many people enter through it. 29

The way leading to life is narrow and the door is narrow as well.
The ones who find it are few. 30

I am the door.
Anyone who enters through me will receive *uddhār* (redemption). 31

The ones who want the praise of people
more than the praise of God did not accept the Lord." 32

Therefore the Lord said:
"The ones who receive praise from each other
but do not search for the praise that comes from God,
how are they able to have *vishwās* (faith)? 33

Those who have made their living from tyranny and prostitution
go into the kingdom of God
before the *dharmachust* (religiously stubborn),
because they have *vishwās*. 34

The *dharmachust āchāryas* and *pandits* (religious teachers)
make God's purpose for their lives worthless." 35

Spiritual knowledge named *Sri Hriday Gitā*;
here ends the tenth chapter named *Mukti*.

Chapter 11
Karmabandhan ane Anugrah
(The Bondage of Karma and Grace)

While going on the road and seeing a man blind from birth,
the shishyas *(disciples) asked:*
"Lord, due to whose *pāp* (sin) was this man born blind?
Who committed *pāp*, he or his parents?" 1

The Lord Jesus said:
"It is not because he or his parents committed *pāp*,
but this happened so the miraculous work of God
may be revealed. 2

While I am in the *jagat* (world),
I am the light of the *jagat*." 3

Speaking thus, the Lord Jesus prepared some clay,
and daubed it on the eyes of the blind man and he was able to see. 4

The Lord said:
"Those eighteen people upon whom the tower fell and killed them;
were they more egregious offenders than everyone else in the city?
You assume this, don't you?
I tell you, it is not so. 5

All have committed *pāp* (sin),
and all remain imperfect before God. 6

'There is no *pāp* in me.' If anyone says this,
then he deceives himself and *satya* (truth/reality) is not in him." 7

Hearing this, a shishya *(disciple) said,*
"The justice of God against evildoers is in accord with *satya*. 8

The one who sins is a violator of *niyam* (law);
He is declared guilty on the basis of *niyam*. 9

Awareness of *pāp* (sin) happens by means of *niyam*.
Through the agency of *niyam*
the stark sinfulness of *pāp* is seen. 10

The one who hears the *niyam* is not *nyāyi* (right) in the sight of God.
Doers of *niyam* are declared *nyāyi*. 11

The one who does not persevere in obeying all the *niyam*
of the *shāstras* (scriptures) is cursed. 12

It is clear that no one is declared *nyāyi* before God
on the basis of *niyam*. 13

So every mouth is closed
and the whole *jagat* (world) is answerable before God. 14

Āgñā (commandments) are *pavitra* (holy), *nyāyi*, and beneficial.
Niyam is *ādhyātmik* (spiritual),
but I am in this body, sold out to *pāp* (sin). 15

When I desire to do good, *pāp* is present.
The *pāp* that dwells within me does the evil." 16

The Lord said:
"Mankind cannot fulfill the *niyam* (law) even when they follow it. 17

Having tried to establish their own *punyashiltā* (meritorious standards),
people have not surrendered to the *punyashiltā* of God. 18

They were seeking to establish this by deeds
and not from *shraddhā* (faith)." 19

A bhakt *said:*
"On the basis of works done according to the rules of life,
no person is declared guiltless. 20

If anyone is declared *nyāyi* (right) before God on the basis of deeds,
then he has reason to be boastful. 21

If a worker gets his salary,
it is not counted to him as *kripā* (grace)
but is counted as a right. 22

Moksh (salvation) is not by means of deeds
lest anyone become proud." 23

At that time the Lord declared this:
"My *kripā* (grace) which brings *mukti* (freedom/salvation)
to all people is revealed." 24

Upon hearing this, the bhakts *(devotees) said:*
"The *dayā* (mercy) of the Lord Jesus, our *uddhārnār* (redeemer),
and his love toward people have been revealed.
Therefore we ourselves are given *uddhār* (redemption),
not through our own *dhārmik karm* (righteous works)
but through his *dayā*. 25

Therefore we have become inheritors of *ananta jivan* (eternal life)
by being declared *nyāyi* (*dhārmik*) [right (lawful/righteous)]*
by his *kripā*. 26

The ones who desire to be declared *nyāyi*
by strict obedience to *niyam* (law) have become averse to *kripā*. 27

_____

dhārmik is in parentheses in the Gujarati text; here the square brackets give our translations of the terms in the
original.

We ourselves are believing in the Lord Jesus,
who is the giver of *anugrah* (grace),
but not based on *karm* (works) done by us. 28

Moksh (salvation) is not of ourselves but is the *dān* (gift) of God.
Therefore, no one can brag before God. 29

Then where is bragging? It has no place,
because *uddhār* (redemption) takes place
through the *anugrah* (grace) of God
by means of *shraddhā* (faith). 30

If it happened through *anugrah*,
then it did not happen through deeds.
Otherwise, *anugrah* is not called *anugrah* at all. 31

The person whom God counts as *nyāyi* (right) apart from deeds,
and the one to whom God does not count *pāp* (sin)
is regarded as blessed." 32

Again the Lord said:
"My *anugrah* is enough for you." 33

A bhakt *said:*
"Let us remain very careful lest anyone miss
receiving the *kripā* (grace) of the Lord. 34

I do not wish to render the *anugrah* of God fruitless. 35

The Lord has delivered us not according to our deeds,
but according to his own *kripā*. 36

That gift comes by *kripā*,
for that gift is received by *vishwās* (faith). 37

We are receiving entrance into this *kripā* by *vishwās*.
Mukti (freedom/salvation) of *ātmā* (spirit) is the fruit of *vishwās*. 38

The Lord Jesus is full of *anugrah*,
and we all from his fullness have received *anugrah* upon *anugrah*." 39

Spiritual knowledge named *Sri Hriday Gitā*;
here ends the eleventh chapter named *Karmabandhan ane Anugrah*.

Chapter 12
Balidānyog (The Yoga of Sacrifice)

The Lord Jesus said:
"I have come that people may have life,
an abundant life." 1

A bhakt *said:*
"Even though you are God, Lord Jesus,
you did not insist on holding on to your *ishwarya* (God-ness). 2

But having assumed the *rup* (form) of a *dās* (servant),
in other words, having come in *manushya* (human) *rup*,
you emptied yourself." 3

The Lord Jesus said:
"I am the *uttam* (good/perfect) shepherd.
The *uttam* shepherd gives his own life for the sheep.
I have come to give my life so people can be set free. 4

My body has been offered for people.
My blood has been poured out for the *māfi* (forgiveness)
of their *pāp* (sins)." 5

At that time, a bhakt *said directly to the Lord Jesus:*
"Behold, the *ishwaryapurush* (God-man)
who carries away the *pāp* of the *jagat* (world)! 6

The one who is *nishkalank* (spotless) and innocent,
the one who is without *pāp*,
has been revealed to carry away *pāp*. 7

91

From one man came *pāp*
and from *pāp* entered death. 8

All people have committed *pāp*, so to all people death spread
and all came under punishment. 9

We all have wandered aimlessly.
Everyone has turned to his own way. 10

He who had not known *pāp*
became *pāprup* (an image of sin) for us
in order that we may become *punyāshiltārup*
(an image of the meritorious standards) of God. 11

The Lord Jesus loved us, and having offered himself,
he himself became a *balidān* (sacrifice). 12

He gave himself as *balidān*
for the *uddhār* (redemption) of all people. 13

He took the weight of all of our *pāp*
and became the *prāyaschitta* (atonement) of our *pāp*. 14

The Lord himself was counted as an offender.
He took the *pāp* of all upon himself,
and impartially mediated for wrong-doers. 15

From his obedience many people are declared *nyāyi* (right).
From his *nyāyi* (righteous) acts
all people have obtained a *nyāyi* life. 16

Due to our *pāp*, he was pierced.
For the obtaining of our *shānti* (peace), he endured punishment. 17

By the *sanātan* (eternal) *ātmā* (spirit)
he gave the spotless *balidān* (sacrifice) of his own self. 18

Having come in the likeness of a body of *pāp* and having
given himself as an *arpan* (offering) for the sake of *pāp*,
he punished *pāp* in his body." 19

Afterward a bhakt *began to say to the Lord:*
"Oh, *swāmi* (master)! In doing so, you are revealing your love to us. 20

You came to banish *pāp* by your *balidān* (sacrifice);
and you willingly offered yourself to bring *uddhār* (redemption)
to all people. 21

Perhaps someone would die for a person
devoted to *dharm* (God's righteous ways);
perhaps someone would dare to die for a moral person. 22

But when we were weak,
you died for us, *adharmis* (people in violation of *dharm*). 23

On the cross in your own body
you took our *pāp* on yourself,
and for our *pāp* you offered *balidān* (sacrifice)." 24

Afterward, a bhakt *said to the* shraddhāvān *(believers):*
"The one who had not known *pāp*
became *pāprup* (image of sin) for our sake. 25

The righteous has suffered in place of the unrighteous. 26

The Lord Jesus who is righteous did *prāyaschitta* (atonement)
for our *pāp* and freed us from the *shrāp* (curse) of the *niyam* (law). 27

He himself became *prāyaschitta*, by which he indicates
his own justice in that, remaining righteous,
he also declares blameless in regard to their *pāp*
those who have *vishwās* (faith). 28

Everyone who has *vishwās* is declared guiltless through him." 29

The Lord Jesus said:
"The one who has *vishwās* in me
will not be declared guilty." 30

A shraddhāvān *(believer) said:*
"Due to the *prāyaschitta* of the Lord Jesus,
according to the riches of his *anugrah* (grace),
we receive *kshamā* (forgiveness) for our crimes. 31

Lord Jesus, you are able to provide *sampurn uddhār* (complete redemption)
to the ones who are surrendering to you. 32

If we all confess our *pāp*,
the Lord is *vishwāsu* (faithful) and *nyāyi* (just)
to give *māfi* (forgiveness) for all our *pāp*,
and to make us *shuddh* (clean) from all our unrighteousness. 33

If we all confess that Christ is Lord,
and in our *hriday* (hearts) keep *shraddhā* (faith) toward him,
then we will receive *moksh* (salvation). 34

He loved us all,
and, by means of his own *balidān* (sacrifice),
he gave us *mukti* (freedom/salvation) from our *pāp*. 35

By means of his *balidān* we have received *kshamā* (forgiveness) of *pāp*.
There is no punishment for those who are in Christ. 36

Homyajña (sacrificial fires) and *arpan* (offerings)
are never powerful enough to remove *pāp*. 37

Therefore, from the once and for all
arpan (offering) of the body of the Lord Jesus Christ
we have all become *pavitra* (holy). 38

He truly performed *balidān* (sacrifice) for *pāp* for all time. 39

From just one *arpan*, the ones who are being made *pavitra*
he has fully perfected for all time." 40

A bhakt *said to the ones who have* shraddhā *(faith):*
"Brothers, the Lord Jesus has opened
a new and living way in his own body for us.
Let us enter into that *pavitrasthān* (holy place). 41

He voluntarily gave himself as *swārpan* (self-offering) for us.
And thus he has given us *uddhār* (redemption) from all unrighteousness. 42

And having made us *pavitra* (holy),
he prepares for himself a special people
eager to do *satkarm* (good works). 43

He did not hold himself back,
but for us he sacrificed himself. 44

So, having shown *dayā* (mercy) to us,
why would he not, with himself, give us all things?" 45

Everyone said:
"To our *parmeshwar pitā* (God and Father) be glory forever.
Tathāstu, tathāstu (amen, amen)." 46

Spiritual knowledge named *Sri Hriday Gitā*;
here ends the twelfth chapter named *Balidānyog*.

Chapter 13
Parampurushyog
(The Yoga of the Supreme Man)

The Lord said:
"First the natural and then the spiritual. 1

The first man from out of the earth is of the soil.
The second man from heaven is the Lord. 2

As the first man is of the soil,
so are the ones who are of the soil. 3

Just as I am the heavenly man,
so also are the ones who are heavenly." 4

A bhakt *said:*
"The first great father became a living being.
The last *parampurush* (supreme man), the Lord Christ,
became a life giving *ātmā* (spirit). 5

From the first great father *pāp* (sin) entered the *jagat* (world),
and from *pāp*, death. 6

All have committed *pāp*,
therefore death has spread to all mankind. 7

This first great father was *pratikrup* (in the likeness) of the *parampurush*. 8

Due to the *pāp* of the first great father, death reigned. 9

In the same way those who receive the *dān* (gift) of *kripā* (grace)
and righteousness from the *parampurush*
will reign in *shāswat jivan* (eternal life). 10

101

We have all been cut out, as it were, from a wild olive tree 11

and have been grafted into a good olive tree.
We have all become partakers of that rich root. 12

We all have become partners of the Lord Christ.
We all are members of the body of the Lord." 13

The Lord Jesus said:
"I give them life.
They remain in me and I remain in them." 14

A bhakt *said:*
"When we all were dead in *pāp* (sin) and crimes,
the Lord made us alive in fellowship with him. 15

We are dead in relation to *pāp*.
Nevertheless, we are alive in relation to the Lord. 16

Because the Lord Christ is within us, the *ātmā* (spirit) is living.
(The *vāsanā* (lusts) of the body are death.) 17

I died, to live for the Lord;
so, now, not I, but Christ lives within me. 18

For the sake of the Lord we are being handed over to death daily,
so the life of the Lord is being revealed in our body of death. 19

As we have received the Lord,
so let us stay in living fellowship with the Lord. 20

The Lord Christ is our life.
Our life has been kept hidden in the Lord. 21

We all have been created in the Lord,
and we all have become partakers in the nature of the Lord. 22

We are the *pratimā* (image) of the Lord
and the *mahimā* (glory) of the Lord. 23

The Lord for all of us has become:
jñān (knowledge), *punyā* (virtue), *pavitratā* (holiness),
and *uddhār* (redemption). 24

That which I am, I am through the *kripā* (grace) of the Lord.
The *kripā* which is upon me is not shown to be fruitless. 25

In the Lord, the *sarva paripurnatā* (complete perfection)
of *ishwaratva* (God-ness) is embodied,
and we all have become *sampurn* (complete) in him." 26

The Lord said:
"I have become glorified in you;
I have given my glory to you." 27

A bhakt *said:*
"May the name of the Lord Jesus be glorified in us,
and let us be glorified in him. 28

The Lord Christ is in us.
He is our hope of glory." 29

Spiritual knowledge named *Sri Hriday Gitā*;
here ends the thirteenth chapter named *Parampurushyog*.

Chapter 14
Samarpanyog (The Yoga of Surrender)

A shāstri *(teacher), drawing near to Jesus, said:*
"Wherever you go
I will follow you." 1

The Lord Jesus said:
"Foxes have dens
and birds have nests,
but I have no place to rest my head." 2

A rich young man, coming to him, asked:
"What should I do to gain *ananta jivan* (eternal life)?" 3

The Lord said to him:
"You are incomplete in one thing:
sell whatever you have, all of it,
give it to the impoverished,
and then come follow me. 4

If any man, having received the whole *duniyā* (world),
loses his own *ātmā* (spirit/life),
then what is the gain to him? 5

If anyone does not renounce all of his possessions,
he cannot be my *shishya* (disciple). 6

The one who loves his father and mother more than me
is not worthy of me. 7

The one who loves his son or daughter more than me
is not worthy of me." 8

A shishya *said:*
"Look, we have given away all our possessions and followed you." 9

The Lord Jesus said:
"If anyone wants to follow me, then he must deny himself
and follow me daily, carrying his cross. 10

Anyone who wishes to save his own life will lose it,
but he who loses his own life for me
will save his own life. 11

If that which we plant does not die, then it does not become alive. 12

If a seed of wheat, having fallen into the soil, does not die it remains alone.
But if it dies, then it produces much fruit. 13

Anyone who loves his own life will lose it,
but the one who hates his own life in this *jagat* (world)
will save it for *ananta jivan* (eternal life)." 14

A shishya *said:*
"It is necessary that the Lord must increase, but I must decrease. 15

I have counted the things that were profitable to me
as loss for the sake of the Lord. 16

For this I suffer all things as a loss,
and count them as rubbish,
so that I may obtain the Lord Jesus. 17

I am not worried about the preciousness of my life,
in order that I may complete the *sevā* (service)
which I have received from the Lord. 18

Every runner in a race runs to get the prize,
nevertheless, only one gets the prize. 19

Let us run the appointed race with patience.
Let us all run in such a way that we get the prize. 20

Let us exercise single-minded devotion towards God. 21

Bodily exercise is somewhat beneficial,
but single-minded devotion to God is beneficial in every way, 22

including blessing both in this present life
and in the life to come. 23

Any soldier going to war is not entangled
in *sansārik* (worldly) affairs. 24

All things are acceptable but not all are beneficial.
All things are acceptable but not all uplift. 25

Everything is permissible to me,
but I will not be enslaved by anything. 26

I have learned to stay content
within my present *āshram* (stage of life).
Let us remain satisfied with the food and clothes we receive." 27

The *mandal* (gathering) of people of *shraddhā* (faith)
was of one *man* (mind) and one way of life.
And they were not saying that their possessions were their own,
but that all things were common to all. 28

No one among them lacked anything
because they were selling their own property
and distributing to all according to anyone's need. 29

A shishya *(disciple) said*:
"Endure the weaknesses of the powerless,
and don't act according to your own happiness.
This is the duty of all of us who are considered strong. 30

Let us bear with each other out of love
in complete meekness, humility and patience." 31

The Lord said:
"The ones who want to walk in the Lord
with *bhaktibhāv* (devotional affection) will be persecuted. 32

Blessed are you when people slander you, attack you,
and falsely speak evil against you for my sake.
Rejoice and be glad. 33

Blessed are you if you are enduring all this
due to full dedication to *dharm* (God's righteous ways). 34

When you endure grief because of doing good,
then in my sight you are worthy of praise. 35

If any person endures injustice and suffers pain
due to *bhaktibhāv*,
then in my sight he is worthy of praise. 36

Endure pain as good soldiers of *swāmi* (master).
Do not be fearful of what you must endure. 37

Whoever I love I reprimand and discipline.
You must endure for the sake of discipline.
No one should waver due to adversity." 38

A shishya *said:*
"The Lord suffered in the flesh for all of us,
so let us also be ready, keeping exactly such a mindset. 39

We all are partakers of the sufferings of the Lord Christ.
Let us rejoice in this. 40

It is not enough to only have *vishwās* (faith) on the Lord Christ,
but also to suffer pain for his sake. 41

What is lacking in the afflictions of the Lord Jesus
I complete in my body. 42

We also rejoice in adversity
because adversity gives birth to patience,
patience to *anubhav* (experiential knowledge),
and *anubhav* to hope. 43

We rejoice exceedingly even though we face
difficult tests through adversity.
We experience grinding poverty, nevertheless rich generosity
is abundantly increasing. 44

114

Although our outer humanity is withering,
nevertheless our inner humanity
is being renewed every single day. 45

Our light and momentary adversity
is creating for us an abundant, unique, eternal weight of glory." 46

The Lord said:
"I know your *kām* (work), your *prem* (love),
your *sevā* (service), your *vishwās* (faith), your *dhiraj* (patience). 47

Remain *vishwāsu* (faithful) to the point of death
and I will give you the crown of life." 48

Spiritual knowledge named *Sri Hriday Gitā*;
here ends the fourteenth chapter named *Samarpanyog*.

Chapter 15
Yajña (Sacrifice), *Tap* (Austerity), and *Dān* (Giving)

The Lord said:
"The ones who are *ādhyātmik* (spiritual) set their *man* (minds)
on *ādhyātmik* things. 1

You have become *pavitra yājak* (holy priests)
to do the *ādhyātmik yajña* (spiritual sacrifices)
which God approves. 2

Having become *pāvan* (pure)
through the *pavitra ātmā* (Holy Spirit),
become an acceptable *arpan* (offering). 3

Offer your bodies, living, *pavitra* (holy) and desirable to the Lord. 4

Let us offer to the Lord continually
a *yajña* (sacrifice) of praise,
that is, to pay homage to his name with the fruit of our lips. 5

Let us not forget to be gracious and distribute *dān* (charitable gifts),
because the Lord is satisfied with such a *yajña*. 6

Dān is certainly a fragrant aroma
and acceptable *arpan* (offering) which the Lord loves." 7

The Lord Jesus said:
"Be careful about doing acts of *dharm* (God's righteous ways)
from a motive of being seen by people. 8

When you fast, do not reveal it to people but do it in secret to God. 9

When you give *dān* (charity), do not let your left hand
know what your right hand gives.
Let your *dāndharm* (dutiful giving) happen in secret. 10

When you give a dinner, summon the poor, crippled, lame and blind
because it is not possible for them to give to you in return." 11

The Lord Jesus saw the rich and powerful giving *dān*
to the *dharmabhandār* (temple treasury),
and saw a poor widow give two paise. 12

At that time the Lord Jesus said:
"This poor widow gave more than all the others 13

because all of them gave a portion from their abundance,
but this poor widow, from her scarcity, donated all that she had. 14

Sell that which you have as an act of *dāndharm*.
Receive for yourself an inexhaustible treasure in heaven. 15

Where your treasure is
there also your *chit* (consciousness/heart) will be. 16

A giver of *dān* should do so from generosity.
He who generously sows will also generously reap. 17

Stay far away from all types of *lobh* (greed).
No one's life consists of their abundant possessions. 18

Lobh for wealth is the root of all types of *pāp* (sin).
Oh *bhakt* (devotee) of God, flee from it!" 19

A bhakt *said:*
"Let us not hope in the uncertainty of wealth, but in the Lord,
who gives us all things richly to enjoy. 20

Let us do good, let us prosper in doing good deeds.
Let us be generous and benevolent. 21

Let us work hard to provide for our necessary expenses.
Having done this, we also ought to assist the needy." 22

The Lord said:
"Don't set your mind on wealth and prosperity,
but with a humble nature be concerned for the poor. 23

It is more blessed to give than to receive.
Care for the poor. 24

Be careful about yourself, otherwise, from excessive consumption
and from the worries of this *sansār* (world),
your *man* (heart) will become hardened. 25

Everyone should care for himself lest he fall into temptation." 26

A bhakt *said:*
"We, taking captive every thought, are obeying the Lord." 27

The Lord Jesus said:
"If your right hand causes you to fall into temptation
then cut it off and throw it away from you. 28

If your right eye causes you to fall into temptation
then gouge it out and throw it away from you. 29

If your eye is pure, then your body is also filled with light.
Be careful that the light which is in you does not become darkness. 30

Be careful about how you listen. 31

Control your tongue.
Let your 'yes' be clearly 'yes'
and let your 'no' be clearly 'no.' 32

Let not a single dirty word leave your mouth,
but only that which is useful for edification.
Your speech should always be attractive and full of *kripā* (grace)." 33

A bhakt *said:*
"We are not like those who please people,
but we speak as those who please the Lord,
the one who examines the *hriday* (heart)." 34

The Lord said:
"The one who thinks he stands firmly
should be careful lest he fall. 35

Be careful with a determined *man* (mind);
be disciplined. 36

Having remained vigilant,
pray that you do not fall into temptation.
The *ātmā* (spirit) is willing but the body is weak. 37

Blessed is the servant whom the master finds awake
when he arrives." 38

A bhakt *said:*
"Every athlete disciplines himself in every way.
I keep my body in control and rule over it. 39

If we all examine ourselves
we will not come under judgment." 40

Spiritual knowledge named *Sri Hriday Gitā*;
here ends the fifteenth chapter named *Yajña*, *Tap* and *Dān*.

Chapter 16
Jñānyog (The Yoga of Knowledge)

The Lord Jesus said:
"This is my will:
that all people obtain the *sampurn jñān* (complete knowledge)
of *satya* (truth/reality) and receive *moksh* (salvation). 1

I give *ananta jivan* (eternal life) to mankind.
Ananta jivan is this; that they know me." 2

A shraddhāvān *(believer) said:*
"Lord, to whom can we go?
You alone have the words of *ananta jivan*." 3

The Lord Jesus said:
"The servant does not know what his master is doing,
but I have called you friends,
and I have made everything known to you. 4

It is not necessary that anyone teach you. 5

My *ātmā* (spirit) resides within you and teaches you all things.
He will reveal to you all that is to come. 6

The *ātmā* of *satya* (truth/reality) will lead you into all *satya*.
I will give you the understanding of all things.
Always increase in knowledge of me." 7

At that time, a shraddhāvān *(believer) said:*
"Glorious Lord, give us the *ātmā* of *buddhi* (wisdom)
and revelation to gain the *jñān* (knowledge)
of *sambandhi* (relationship) with you, 8

so we can be filled
with the *jñān* of God's will
in all spiritual understanding and *buddhi*. 9

Let us determine what is best, so our love increases
more and more in *jñān* and *vivek* (discernment). 10

Let us increase in the *jñān* of our *tāranhār* (savior) and *swāmi* (master).
May the word of the Lord abundantly dwell within us
through *sarva jñān* (all knowledge). 11

Oh, Lord! How unfathomable
are the riches of your *buddhi* (wisdom) and *jñān*!
How incomprehensible are your decrees!
And how mysterious are your ways! 12

Due to the excellencies of the *jñān* of my Lord,
I count all my gain as rubbish. 13

We are unable to do anything against *satya* (truth/reality),
but we are doing everything for the defense of *satya*. 14

Because we have come to know the Lord,
he has given us all things pertaining to
life and *bhaktibhāv* (devotional affection). 15

Because we have come to know the Lord,
kripā (grace) and *shānti* (peace) have abundantly come upon us." 16

The Lord said:
"The one who says I know God
but does not obey the commands of God lies,
and *satya* (truth/reality) is not in him. 17

The one who commits *pāp* (sin) has not seen God
and does not know him. 18

He walks in the delusion of his own *man* (mind)
and due to his *buddhi* (intellect) having become darkened
and from the hardening of his *hriday* (heart),
he becomes *ajñān* (ignorant).
Therefore he is far from an *ishwariy* (godly) life. 19

He is pretending to know about God
but by his deeds he denies him. 20

Be careful lest someone entangle you in empty philosophy
that is according to the traditions of men
and according to the elementary principles of *sansār* (the world). 21

The *jagat* (world) has not known God
by its own *jñān* (knowledge). 22

Such *jñān* swells up arrogantly, but love edifies. 23

Love is from God.
If anyone loves God,
then he knows God. 24

Sansārik (worldly) people are not accepting
my *ādhyātmik* (spiritual) words
because these words are foolishness to them. 25

They are understood in an *ādhyātmik* way,
so he is unable to understand them. 26

No one understands the word of God
without the *ātmā* (Spirit) of God." 27

At that time a shraddhāvān *(believer) said:*
"Lord, you kept these words hidden from *jñānis* (scholars)
and *tarkashāstris* (philosophers).
You, Lord, have revealed them to children. 28

Who has known the *man* (mind) of God?
But we have the *man* of the Lord Jesus. 29

We have received the *ātmā* from the Lord
that we may know the things which the Lord has given us. 30

By revelation the Lord has made known to me the mystery. 31

The Lord who commanded light to shine out of darkness
has shone in our *hriday* (hearts),
to give the light of the *jñān* (knowledge) of his glory. 32

Things which eye has not seen and ear has not heard,
these things which have not entered the *man* (mind) of people,
the Lord has revealed to us from his own *ātmā*." 33

The Lord said:
"The *jñān* (knowledge) which comes from me is calm,
conciliatory, humble, easily understood,
full of *dayā* (mercy) and good fruit,
impartial, and devoid of hypocrisy. 34

A *jñāni* (learned man) is proven right
by his good works done in humility
and good behaviour through *jñān*. 35

Whoever hears my teaching and understands it,
and from a clean and good *dil* (heart)
receives the word, patiently bears fruit. 36

131

Determine what the Lord approves.
Understand what the Lord desires.
Learn from me." 37

In one village, two sisters entertained the Lord in their home. 38

The younger sister sat at the feet of the Lord
and listened to the teaching of the Lord.
But the older sister was anxious because there was so much work. 39

She said to the Lord:
"Lord, my sister has abandoned me to do all of the work alone." 40

The Lord said to her:
"You are anxious and fearful about many teachings
but one teaching is needful, 41

and your sister has chosen the good part
which will not be taken away from her." 42

At that time the shishyas *(disciples) said:*
"We all know that the Lord has come
and has given us understanding
to know the one who is *satya* (truth/reality). 43

We are in that one who is truthful.
He alone is the true God and *ananta jivan* (eternal life)." 44

Spiritual knowledge named *Sri Hriday Gita*;
here ends the sixteenth chapter named *Jñānyog*.

Chapter 17
Vishuddhiyog (The Yoga of Purification)

The Lord said:
"I am *pavitra* (holy), so you be *pavitra*." 1

A shraddhāvān *(believer) said:*
"The one who called us is *pavitra*,
so let all of us also be *pavitra* in all manner of behavior. 2

Let us be *shuddh* (pure) by removing all filthiness
of the body and *ātmā* (spirit).
Let us attain the full measure of *pavitratā* (holiness),
fearing the Lord. 3

Let us make an effort to stay in *shānti* (peace) by being innocent
and spotless in the sight of the Lord." 4

The Lord Jesus said:
"I am the vine and you are the branches."
With harsh *(gladness) a* shraddhāvān *(believer) said:*
"If the root is *pavitra* (holy) then the branches are *pavitra* also." 5

The Lord said:
"You have obeyed the *satya* (truth/reality)
and made your *man* (heart) *pavitra*.
By *vishwās* (faith) your *man* (hearts) are being made *pavitra*. 6

If anyone remains *shuddh* (pure) from vile deeds,
then he will be a *pavitra* vessel prepared for noble use,
consecrated and helpful to *swāmi* (the master)." 7

At that time a shraddhāvān *(believer) said:*
"The Lord makes us *shuddh* from all *pāp* (sin).
The one who takes the name of the Lord must stay away from *pāp*. 8

Let us all keep ourselves spotless from *sansār* (the world).
Let us always try to keep a guiltless *antahkaran* (conscience)
before God and men. 9

Let us calm our *antahkaran* before God about anything
in which our *antahkaran* accuses us 10

because he is greater than our *antahkaran* and knows all things. 11

The Lord disciplines us for our good
so we may become partakers in *pavitratā* (holiness). 12

God, giver of *shānti* (peace), make us *purā pavitra* (completely holy)
and keep our *ātmā* (spirit), *prān* (life),
and *sharir* (body) in complete purity. 13

And, Lord, present us *pavitra*, spotless
and guiltless in your presence." 14

The Lord said:
"In the midst of fraudulent and obstinate people show yourselves
guiltless, honest and spotless children of God,
as lights in the *jagat* (world). 15

Once having become *pavitra* (holy), *pāp* (sin) does not control again
the *antahkaran* (inner being) of *bhakts* (devotees).
To the *shuddh* (pure) in *man* (heart), everything is *shuddh*. 16

Having been given *mukti* (freedom/salvation) from *pāp*
and having become a *dās* (servant) of the Lord
you are becoming *pavitra*,
and as a result you receive *ananta jivan* (eternal life)." 17

Spiritual knowledge named *Sri Hriday Gitā*;
here ends the seventeenth chapter named *Vishuddhiyog*.

Chapter 18
Purnyog (The Perfect Yoga)

A shishya *(disciple) said*:
"In the Lord Jesus dwells all *sampurnatā* (perfection).
Let us all grow towards *sampurnatā*. 1

Let us all arrive at the threshold of the *sampurnatā* of the Lord Jesus
in mature *purushatva* (humanness). 2

Lord, by means of your *ātmā* (spirit),
make us strong in our inner being
so that we may become *sampurn* (perfect)
according to all the *sampurnatā* of the Lord. 3

Lord, make us *sampurn* in every good work so that we do all
according to your will and do that which is pleasing in your sight. 4

Lord, make *sampurn* our desire for good
and our works of *shraddhā* (faith). 5

Up to now I have not acquired everything,
nor have I become *sampurn*. 6

But, forgetting that which is behind,
and running toward that which is before,
I push forward towards the mark
for the prize of the heavenly calling. 7

The Lord has given us all things pertaining to
life and *bhaktibhāv* (devotional affection). 8

For this reason make every effort to supplement your *vishwās* (faith)
with *chāritra* (virtue), 9

chāritra with *jñān* (knowledge), *jñān* with *sayam* (self control), 10

sayam with *dhiraj* (patience),
dhiraj with *bhaktibhāv* (devotional affection), 11

bhaktibhāu with *bandhubhāv* (familial affection),
and *bandhubhāv* with *prem* (love). 12

That which is *satya* (true/real), that which is worthy of respect,
that which is *nyāyi* (right), that which is *shuddh* (pure),
that which is worthy of love,
that which is admirable; 13

if anything is virtuous, and if anything is praiseworthy,
then let us think on these things. 14

As the chosen people of the Lord let us embrace
tenderness of *hriday* (heart), gentleness, humility,
respectful behaviour and patience. 15

The Lord has given us *ashirvād* (blessing)
with every *ādhyātmik* (spiritual) *ashirvād*. 16

Seek the things which are above.
Direct your *chit* (consciousness) to things above. 17

May the will of the Lord be done on earth as it is in heaven. 18

Not according to my will,
but may it be according to the Lord's will." 19

The Lord said:
"Stand firm by being *sampurn* (perfect)
and by having full assurance of the will of the Lord. 20

God-inspired scripture is useful for teaching,
so the *bhakts* (devotees) of God become *sampurn*
and become ready for *sarva satkarm* (all good works). 21

Be ready to make *sampurn* the *sevā* (service)
which has been given to you. 22

Let patience fully conclude its work in you
so you may be totally mature and *sampurn*, not lacking in anything. 23

Endure for a short time
and then I myself will make you
purn (complete), stable and strong. 24

May my *shānti* (peace) reign in your *hriday* (heart).
My *shānti* will protect your *man* (mind) and *hriday*." 25

A shishya *said:*
"As the heavenly Father is *purn*, so let us all be *purn*. 26

The one who began a good work in us will make it *sampurn*. 27

When I was a child, I spoke as a child, I thought as a child,
I understood as a child. 28

But, when I grew up, I put away childish things.
When *sampurnatā* (perfection) comes,
then *apurnatā* (imperfection) will vanish." 29

Spiritual knowledge named *Sri Hriday Gitā*;
here ends the eighteenth chapter named *Purnyog*.

Chapter 19
Vibhutiyog
(The Yoga of Universal Lordship)

The Lord Jesus said:
"I am the beginning, the middle, and the end.
Everything was created by me.
I created all of the worlds.
That which is, has not been created without me. 1

I am the cause of the entire created order.
All things are through me, by me and for me." 2

A bhakt *said:*
"Oh Lord, the heavens are your handiwork.
In the beginning, you laid the foundation of the earth. 3

As a garment they will be changed, but you are unchanging.
Your reign will never end." 4

The Lord said:
"I am above all, among all, and in all.
With my powerful word I maintain all things.
I give life and breath to all living beings. 5

I am *satya* (truth/reality) and life.
I am not far from anyone because all are alive in me.
In me all live, move and exist." 6

A shraddhāvān *(believer) said:*
"Lord, everything is from you and we exist for your sake.
Everything depends on you, and we all depend on you. 7

According to your resolve and desire you do all things.
Who can hinder your plans? 8

You are the one who fills everyone with all things.
You are 'Emmanuel' which means 'God who lives with us'." 9

The Lord said:
"Nothing created is hidden from my sight.
I am the knower of the thoughts and feelings of the *hriday* (heart),
and of the *man* (mind) and *antahkaran* (conscience). 10

I am the same yesterday, today and forever;
he who was, he who is, and he who is coming. 11

I am the introduction and the conclusion, the first and the last,
the beginning and the end. 12

In me dwells the *sampurnatā* (completeness) of all things.
In me are hidden all treasures of *jñān* (knowledge)
and *buddhi* (wisdom). 13

I am *jñān*, *punya* (merit), *pavitratā* (holiness), and *uddhār* (redemption).
That which is *pavitra* (holy), that which is *satya* (true/real),
that which is *tathāstu* (amen), that which is *vishwāsniya* (faithful),
I am." 14

A shraddhāvān *(believer) said:*
"Oh Lord, your invisible attributes, eternal power,
and *ishwaratva* (God-ness) are obvious
from observations of created things." 15

The Lord said:
"That which is in the sky, that which is in the earth,
that which is visible and invisible; thrones and kingdoms,
rulers and authorities are all created through me and for me. 16

I am before all things and through me all remains well ordered." 17

A bhakt *lifted his voice and said:*
"The messengers of God (angels) all do your *bhajan* (worship).
You make your messengers in the form of wind,
and your servants in the form of flame." 18

The Lord said:
"All authority is mine in heaven and on earth. 19

I have the keys to death and the underworld.
I open, and no one will close. I close and no one opens. 20

I am the head over kingdoms and authorities.
Through my power, I am able to bring all into subjection to me." 21

At that time a shraddhāvān *(believer) said:*
"You are preeminent over all. 22

O God, your kingdom is eternal
and your rule is the scepter of justice. 23

You, blessed and unique *swāmi* (master),
are king of kings and *swāmi* of *swāmis*. 24

You are the ruler of all ages
and of the kingdom which will never end. 25

The kingdom, power, and glory are yours alone forever. 26

All in heaven, on the earth, and beneath the earth,
will bow prostrate at your name, and every tongue will confess
that you alone are *swāmi*." 27

The Lord said:
"I dwell in incomprehensible light.
I myself am light and the father of lights. 28

The one who commanded glorious light to shine from the darkness
has caused the light to shine in the *hriday* (heart) of people. 29

I am the *mārg* (way), the *satya* (truth/reality), and the *jivan* (life).
I am *shāswat jivan* (eternal life). Mine alone is immortality.
I have revealed life and immortality. 30

I am the living *roti* (bread) which descended from heaven.
The one who comes to me will never hunger again. 31

Whoever drinks the water that I give will never thirst again." 32

Spiritual knowledge named *Sri Hriday Gitā*;
here ends the nineteenth chapter named *Vibhutiyog*.

Chapter 20
Brihadrup (The Greater Body)

The Lord Jesus said:
"Where two or three are united together in my name
I am present in their midst. 1

I am the vine and you are the branches." 2

A bhakt *said:*
"As the body is one and its members are many,
and as there are many members of the body,
yet together they form one body,
so also is Christ the Lord. 3

We are the body of the Lord and his various members.
As there are many members in our body,
and not all the members do the same task, 4

similarly, although we are many, yet in the Lord we are one body
and mutually members of one another. 5

Āryan (noble) or non *āryan* (ignoble), *dās* (slave) or *swatantra* (free),
we all have received *sanskār* (initiation) from one *ātmā* (spirit),
and have become one body. 6

They who were distant and the ones who were near,
the Lord has made them all one.
And having reconciled in himself the two into one
has created one new humanity. 7

Now there is no *āryan* or non *āryan*, there is no circumcised
or uncircumcised, there is no male or female,
because we are all one in Christ the Lord. 8

The Lord Christ is all and is in all. He is our life. 9

If any person is in the Lord he is a new beginning, a new creation. 10

The Lord has arranged every member in the body
in accordance with his own desire. 11

The whole body is arranged by him and every joint is connected;
every part works according to its own strength to grow in love
for the edification of the body." 12

The Lord said:
"I am the head of the body. The whole body grows
by receiving nourishment from the head which is joined to it." 13

A bhakt *said:*
"Let us grow in every way through Christ who is the head
by lovingly following *satya* (truth/reality). 14

If all were the same member, then where would the body be?
The members are many, but the body is one.
We are many, nevertheless we are one body. 15

The Lord has arranged the body in such an orderly fashion
that discord does not happen in the body.
Rather, all the members keep common concern for each other. 16

If one member feels pain,
then all the members feel pain with him. 17

In the same way, if one member is respected
then all the members rejoice with him. 18

There are various kinds of *dān* (gifts) of *kripā* (grace),
yet there is only one *ātmā* (spirit).
There are various kinds of *sevā* (service), but there is only one Lord.
There are various kinds of works, but only one Lord,
who is the absolute ruler in everything. 19

According to his own will he distributed different *dān* to each.
The doer of all this is the *pavitra ātma* (Holy Spirit). 20

The revelation of the *pavitra ātma* is given for the good of all. 21

Our bodies are the members of the Lord.
There is one body and one *ātmā* (spirit),
one Lord who is above all, among all, and in all." 22

The Lord said:
"I have given you my glory for you to be one.
I dwell in you so that you become *sampurn* (complete) and united." 23

At that time a bhakt *said:*
"The Lord has made known to us the mystery of his will,
that in the arrangement of the *sampurnatā* (completeness) of time,
he would unite all things in heaven and on earth in himself. 24

Therefore, whatever may be on earth
and whatever may be in heaven,
he is reconciling it all with himself." 25

Spiritual knowledge named *Sri Hriday Gitā*;
here ends the twentieth chapter named *Brihadrup*.

Chapter 21
Daivasur Sampad
(Conflict between Good and Evil)

The Lord said:
"Do not love *sansār* (the world) or the things within *sansār*.
If anyone loves *sansār*, then he has no love for me. 1

All that is in *sansār*, such as bodily *vāsanā* (lust), desire of the eyes,
and the arrogance of life, is not from me but is from *sansār*. 2

Sansār and its craving vanishes,
but the one who fulfills my desire remains forever." 3

A bhakt *said:*
"Friendship with *sansār* is enmity towards God.
Anyone who wishes to be a friend of *sansār*
becomes an enemy of God." 4

The Lord Jesus said:
"Do not be astonished if *sansār* hates you.
You are not of *sansār*, but I have chosen you out of *sansār*. 5

You are in this *jagat* (world), but not of this *sansār*.
I do not desire that you be removed from *jagat*,
but I desire that you be protected from *pāp* (sin). 6

You have adversity in *sansār*, but be courageous;
I have triumphed over *sansār*. 7

He who is within you is greater than that which is in *sansār*." 8

A shraddhāvān *(believer) said:*
"The one who is born of God defeats *sansār*.
Our *vishwās* (faith) is the victory which has triumphed over *sansār*. 9

I am crucified to *sansār* and *sansār* is crucified to me." 10

The Lord said:
"Bodily passions fight against *ātmā* (spirit).
As a foreigner and traveler in this life, stay far away from them. 11

Do not be obsessed with the *durvāsanā* (evil lusts) of the body.
Kill the deeds of bodily *vāsanā* (lusts) by means of *ātmā*. 12

Don't be overcome by evil but overcome evil with good. 13

Hate what is evil, cling to what is good. 14

I have been revealed to destroy
the works of *dusht ātmā* (the evil spirit). 15

Evil does not touch the one who is born of God.
You are strong and have overcome the evil one." 16

A shraddhāvān *(believer) said:*
"The Lord is *vishwāsniya* (faithful) and will strengthen us
and protect us from evil. 17

The Lord knows how to free *bhakts* (devotees) from temptation. 18
The Lord will protect us from every evil attack

and will keep us safe and sound for his heavenly kingdom." 19

The Lord said:
"Your war is not with flesh and blood but against rulers
and against authorities and against dark powers
of *sansār* (the world) and against evil *ādhyātmik* (spiritual) forces. 20

Therefore, equip yourself against them with all the weapons of God,
and having done all, you will be able to stand firm. 21

Bind your waist with *satya* (truth/reality).
Wear the armour of righteousness.
Seize the shield of *shraddhā* (faith),
and take the *ādhyātmik* sword of the word of God. 22

The one who triumphs I will set on my throne with me." 23

A bhakt *said*:
"God is light and in him there is no darkness.
That light, having come into the *jagat* (world),
gives light to every person. 24

The one who does evil hates the light and does not come near the light, but the one who does *satya* comes near the light." 25

The Lord said:
"As long as you have light, walk in the light,
lest the darkness fall upon you. 26

What relationship do light and darkness have?
Light reveals all that is worthy of contempt. 27

Do not join in with fruitless deeds of darkness, instead expose them.
The fruit of light is in all goodness, justice and *satya*. 28

You are the light of the *jagat* (world).
Let your light shine before people so that they,
having seen your gracious works, may praise me." 29

A bhakt *said*:
"Let us reveal the virtues of the Lord who has invited us
into his marvelous light, out of darkness." 30

The Lord said:
"I have eradicated death and revealed life and immortality." 31

A shraddhāvān *(believer) said:*
"Death is the last enemy to be destroyed.
The sting of death is *pāp* (sin), but we triumph through our Lord. 32

Oh death, where is your sting?
Oh death, where is your victory?" 33

Spiritual knowledge named *Sri Hriday Gitā*;
here ends the twenty-first chapter named *Daivasur Sampad*.

Chapter 22
Pralay (Destruction)

The Lord said:
"God blesses the land which constantly absorbs rain
and produces useful plants for the farmer. 1

But he rejects land upon which thorns and prickly shrubs grow.
That land is cursed and consequently is burned up completely. 2

Every tree that does not bear good fruit is cut down
and thrown into the fire." 3

A bhakt said:
"The Lord has not failed to give a witness about himself
by prosperous and fruitful seasons from heaven
and by satisfying our *man* (hearts) with daily food and *ānand* (joy). 4

The favour of God inspires us to repentance.
By being ignorant, do you consider worthless his favour,
forbearance, and abundant riches of patience? 5

He was in the *jagat* (world), and he created the *jagat*,
yet the *jagat* did not recognize him. 6

He came to his own people, but his own people did not accept him. 7

Are you, through your hard and impenitent *antahkaran* (hearts),
accumulating great wrath for yourselves
to be certainly revealed on the day of the judgment day of God?" 8

The Lord said:
"The *niyam* (law) is written on everyone's *antahkaran* (conscience)
and their *buddhi* (mind) confirms it." 9

A shraddhāvān *(believer) said:*
"The Lord will reveal in the open what is said
in the secret of darkness, and the intentions of the *hriday* (heart). 10

The wrath of God has been revealed from heaven
against the *adharmipanu* (lawlessness)
and evil deeds of those people
who suppress *satya* (truth/reality) with evil. 11

Those who have not accepted *satya*
with love for their *moksh* (salvation),
who have not had *vishwās* (faith) in *satya*,
but who rejoice in *adharm* (lawlessness), will be condemned. 12

Those who do not know the Lord and do not accept his good news
will suffer eternal destruction, that is,
the punishment of banishment from the presence of the Lord. 13

167

If we are careless about the *mahānuddhār* (great redemption),
then how can we escape?
It is terrible to fall into the hands of the living God. 14

Because if we knowingly commit *pāp* (sin)
after we have *jñān* (knowledge) of *satya*,
all that remains is the terrible expectation
of judgment and the wrath of consuming fire. 15

When they say 'peace and safety' they will suddenly be destroyed,
as birth pangs come on a woman. 16

The Lord does not delay in relation to his word.
But desiring that no one perish but all repent,
the Lord is patient with us. 17

The Lord has endured with great patience
those who deserve destruction and are worthy of wrath.
Accept that the patience of the Lord is *uddhār* (redemption). 18

The present heaven and earth have been kept ready
for the day of destruction of *adhārmik* (lawless) people by fire. 19

At that time the heavens will disappear with a great thunderous roar;
the elements will melt, and the earth and all it contains
will be totally burned. 20

All of this will be destroyed, so what should we become
in our *pavitra* (holy) behaviour
and our *bhaktibhāv* (attitude of devotion)? 21

See the Lord's goodness as well as his severity;
do not be arrogant but fearful." 22

The Lord said:
"The Lord is opposed to the proud but bestows *dayā* (mercy)
on humble people, so obey me." 23

A shraddhāvān *(believer) said:*
"Oh, *sarvashaktimān* (almighty) Lord God!
Your works are great and wonderful. 24

Oh, king of the *yugs* (ages)!
Your way is *nyāyi* (right) and *satya* (true/real).
Oh, Lord, who will not fear you?" 25

The Lord said:
"The law-giver and the judge are one.
He is *shaktimān* (powerful) to save and to destroy." 26

A shraddhāvān *(believer) said:*
"Oh, Lord, you alone are the one who saves us
from the wrath to come." 27

The Lord said:
"I will save you from the time of testing
that is coming on the entire *sansār* (world) 28

because you are appointed for *uddhār* (redemption)
by me, not for wrath." 29

Spiritual knowledge named *Sri Hriday Gitā*;
here ends the twenty-second chapter named *Pralay*.

Chapter 23
Paramgati (Ultimate Freedom)

The Lord said:
"If anyone does my *sevā* (service) then he must follow me,
and where I am, there my *sevak* (servant) will also stay." 1

A bhakt *said:*
"The Lord has seated us in heavenly places with himself
and has given us *ashirvād* (blessing)
with every *ādhyātmik* (spiritual) *ashirvād* in the heavenlies. 2

We do not have a permanent city in which to dwell here,
but we anticipate our city which is to come. 3

The Lord has prepared a city for us.
Its planner and builder is God.
We hope for it. 4

We are waiting for a new heaven and new earth
according to the word of the Lord, in which justice dwells.
Our citizenship is in heaven. 5

The creation waits expectantly
for the revelation of the children of God. 6

The creation itself having been given *mukti* (freedom/salvation)
from the bondage of destruction,
hopes to join in the glorious *mukti* (freedom/salvation)
of the children of God." 7

The Lord said:
"See! I make all things new!" 8

A shraddhāvān *(believer) said:*
"Earthly people are not able to inherit the heavenly kingdom;
the corruptible does not inherit the incorruptible. 9

As we all have assumed an earthen *pratimā* (image),
so we also will assume a heavenly *pratimā*. 10

Now we all see dimly, but then we will see face to face. 11

Now I do not know completely,
but then I will know as I myself am known. 12

Now we are all the offspring of God,
and what we will be is not yet revealed. 13

When the Lord will be revealed, we will become like him.
As he is heavenly, so also we will be heavenly. 14

If that which is passing away is glorious,
that which is permanent has far surpassing glory." 15

The Lord said:
"I will bring you to myself so that where I am,
there you may also stay with me." 16

At that time a bhakt *and* shraddhāvān *(believers) said as one:*
"The Lord is powerful to place us
in his presence with *param* (supreme) *ānand* (joy). 17

The Lord has made us partakers
in the inheritance of the saints in light. 18

There will be no night there.
The light of the moon or sun is not needed there
because the glory of God is its light. 19

The Lord himself will shine on us
and we will stay with the Lord forever. 20

Things which eye has not seen, ear has not heard
nor has entered the *man* (minds) of people, 21

is what the Lord has appointed for those who love him. 22

At that time the righteous ones will shine like the sun
in the kingdom of the Father." 23

Conclusion

The Lord said:
"Many were desiring to see what you see
but it was not given to them to see,
and many were desiring to hear what you hear
but it was not given to them to hear. 24

Blessed are those who hear my word and obey it. 25

If anyone desires to fulfill the will of God,
then he will understand this teaching. 26

I am with you always, until the end of the *jagat* (world).
Receive *shānti* (peace), receive *shānti,* receive *shānti.*" 27

A bhakt *said:*
"He who hears this word, must receive it
not as the word of man
but as it is, the word of God. 28

The one who is of God hears the word of God. 29

These sayings are worthy of *vishwās* (faith)
and *satya* (truth/reality).
The word of the Lord is living and forever enduring.
No word of the Lord fails to achieve its purpose. 30

Blessed is the one who has *vishwās*,
for the word that has come from the Lord will be fulfilled." 31

Tathāstu (Amen)

Spiritual knowledge named *Sri Hriday Gitā*;
here ends the twenty-third chapter named *Paramgati*.

Sri Hriday Gitā is concluded.

Appendix

Dhanjibhai Fakirbhai (1895-1967) first produced this introduction to and interpretation of Jesus Christ in Gujarati in the mid 1950s.[1] Dhanjibhai was born and raised as a Hindu and became a disciple of Jesus in his early years. As a disciple of Jesus he identified with Christianity and joined the Methodist Church, but Dhanjibhai was one of many who recognized that Jesus does not belong to Christianity. So he wrote a number of striking books, including this one, introducing and interpreting Jesus for his Gujarati Hindu world

An English edition of this book was produced in the late 1960s by Indian Christians who were impressed by Dhanjibhai's creative interpretation. They decided, however, against actually translating Dhanjibhai's creative paraphrases and instead used the exact terminology

---

1. Robin H. S. Boyd prepared a scholarly introduction to Dhanjibhai and his works, *Manilal C. Parekh, 1885 1967, Dhanjibhai Fakirbhai, 1895-1967: A Selection*, edited and introduced by Robin H. S. Boyd, Madras Christian Literature Society for the Dept. of Research and Post-graduate Studies, United Theological College Bangalore, 1974.

of the English Bible. This resulted in a very different book than that which Dhanjibhai had written.[2]

The translators felt deeply the challenge of their task, and confess the inadequacy of their work. The Gujarati language Dhanjibhai used to write about Jesus is a Sanskrit-based north Indian language.[3] The Sanskritic languages have rich resources for speaking of God and the spirit, yet the very richness of terms available complicates translation. Early twenty-first century English has already absorbed numerous Sanskrit words into its working vocabulary, such as guru, karma and dharma. The transplanting of these terms into English has continued the transformation of meaning of those terms, as all words in all living languages and traditions have continually shifting meanings and connotations, usually rather subtly but at times quite radically.

---

2. *Shri Khrist Gita: The Song of the Lord Christ*, Dhanjibhai Fakirbhai, Delhi: Unity Books, 1969. This edition was also reprinted in England a few decades later.

3. At a few points Dhanjibhai uses terms of Persian rather than Sanskrit origin; he was a gifted communicator who was not bound by artificial standards of linguistic propriety. Persian-based terms are indicated as such in the glossary.

In this work not only the newly English-ized Sanskrit terms just mentioned, but many other rich Sanskritic terms have been adopted into the English text, with English meanings in parentheses. Christians easily become tethered to particular phrases of the Bible, and some might feel scandalized by this process. But the scandal of translation is central to the Bible, and needs to be embraced. Precious few words of Jesus are extant, those being the handful of words or phrases of Aramaic (the language Jesus spoke) that have slipped into the New Testament of the Bible. Otherwise, all the words of Jesus accessible today are translated words. The New Testament that introduces Jesus was written in Greek, so a massive translation and interpretation had already taken place between the speaking of Jesus and the recording of his message. Further translations from Greek into thousands of languages around the world bring further transformation of the original phraseology and meaning of Jesus.

Yet among the riches of translations of Jesus and the New Testament this current book perhaps can claim a unique niche. Dhanjibhai did not produce a new translation of the New Testament or of the words of Jesus, he presented a rich paraphrase and reinterpretation of the message of Jesus into a Sanskritic language where Jesus is still not at home. Translating back from Gujarati to the English language that was so formatively influenced by the Bible highlights the complexity of communication and translation.[4] Almost surely this dynamic influenced the earlier decision to produce an English edition of this book that merely used standard Bible words rather than attempt what this edition attempts.

A page or more could be written about translators' decisions in each chapter of this book, but that would interrupt the creative dynamic Dhanjibhai undertook, which we desire to reproduce in significant measure in this English edition.[5] One further matter does need comment, however. In quite a few places Dhanjibhai attributes to the Lord statements which in the New Testament are from the apostles of Jesus and not Jesus himself. The translators were never tempted to "correct" these "errors" since Dhanjibhai clearly knew the New Testament and knew he was "falsely" attributing some of his paraphrases. Other than for stylistic reasons, we have no explanation for this phenomenon in our text which we faithfully translate.

The translators
March 2014

---

4. Various Gujarati editions of Dhanjibhai's text are also available, and along with differences there are clear errors in those printed texts; establishing a best Gujarati text for this work was beyond the mandate of this present project.

5. We also at times referenced the Hindi translation of this work, but we were not impressed with the Hindi edition and hope to see a better translation into Hindi produced at some future time.

Glossary

āchārya spiritual leader or guide, a teacher, a man of learning
adharm not in accord with dharma, unrighteousness, irreligion, sin, immorality, action contrary to the scriptures
adhārmik lawless, unrighteous, irreligious
adharmipanu lawlessness
ādhyātmik spiritual
āgñā commandments
ajñān ignorant, without knowledge
akhand without lack, complete, unbroken, undivided
amaratva immortality
ānand joy
ananta unending, eternal
ane and

antahkaran inner being, soul, heart, mind, conscience
antar inside, inner, internal, soul, heart
anubhav experience, direct knowledge, proved
anugrah grace, favour, kindness, obligation, mercy
aprādh wrongdoing
arpan offering, giving, dedication
āryan noble, civilized, of the Aryan civilization
āshram stage of life
ātmā spirit or self, life, principle of life, supreme being, original substance
avatār descent, particularly the descent of God into this world

balidān sacrifice, offering of oblation to God
bandhubhāv familial affection, brotherly love
bhajan a style of spiritual song, praise songs to God, singing praise to God
bhakt devotee
bhakti devotion
bhaktibhāv devotional affection
buddhi intellect, discriminatory faculty, sense, understanding, wisdom

chākar servant (menial)
chāritra virtue, good character, strength of character
chit consciousness, heart, mind, attention, life, spirit, soul

dān giving, charity, donation
dāndharm dutiful giving
darshan vision, often spiritual vision; also used for philosophy
dās servant, slave
dayā mercy
devadut messenger of God, angel
dharm God's righteous ways, knowledge, morality, good behavior, religion, one's
    duty
dharmabhandār temple treasury
dharmachust religiously stubborn, devoted to one's own religion, orthodox, strict
dhārmik righteous, dutiful
dhiraj patience
dil heart (Persian origin)
divya heavenly, divine, wonderful, shining

diyā lamp
duniyā world (Persian origin)
durvāsanā evil inclination, lust
dusht evil

ekrup one, of the same shape or size, identical

gitā song

harsh gladness, joy, happiness
homyajña sacrificial fires
hriday heart

ishwaratva God-ness
ishwarya God-ness
ishwaryapurush God(*ishwar*)-man(*purush*)

jagat world
jāti people, caste, community
jivan life
jñān knowledge, wisdom
jñāni scholar, enlightened one

kām work
karm works, deeds, function, conduct, religious ceremony, fate, deeds of past lives
karmabandhan bondage of karma
khās special (Persian origin)
kripā grace
kripāsan gracious throne
kshamā forgiveness

lobh greed
lok people

māfi forgiveness (Persian origin)
mahān great
mahānuddhār great redemption, uplift, emancipation, deliverance
mahimā glory, greatness, majesty, exalted rank or position
man soul, heart, mind
mandal gathering, circle
mandir temple
manushyarup human/man (*manushya*) form (*rup*)
mārg way, path, mode, creed, religious sect, guidance
moksh salvation, liberation, emancipation
mukti freedom, salvation, emancipation, liberation, release

nishkalank spotless
niyam law
nyāyi right, righteous, just

pandit teacher, often used as synonym for Brahman

pāp sin, trouble, calamity

pāpi sinner, sinful

param supreme

paramātmā Supreme Spirit (God)

parampurush supreme man

paripurnatā perfection

parmeshwar God, Supreme God

paschyātāp repentance, penitence

pāvan holy, spiritually pure

pavitra holy, pure, clean, sacred

pavitrasthān holy place, pure place, sacred place

pavitratā holiness, purity

pitā father

prabhutā deity (lit., lord (*prabhu*)-ness(*tā*))

prajā people, a people group, subjects

prakāshrup light (lit., form (*rup*) of light (*prakāsh*))

prākritik natural

prān life, breath, soul, strength, vigor
pratikrup image
pratimā image, idol, resemblance
prāyaschitt sacrifice of atonement
prem love
punarjanma re-birth, in many contexts reincarnation, new birth
punyā virtue, merit, righteous, righteous deeds
punyashiltā meritorious standards
purā complete
purn complete, all
purushatva humanness

rāj king, kingdom
rup fɔrm, shape, appearance

sād voice
sambandh relationship

samarpan surrender, offering, surrendering oneself to one's spiritual guide or to God

sampurn fully complete

sampurnatā perfection, completeness

sanātan eternal

sansār world, universe, worldly life, cycle of birth and death, domestic life

sansārik worldly, relating to worldly affairs, being involved in domestic life

sarva all

sarvashaktimān almighty

satkarm good works

satya truth, reality

satyatā truth (lit., truth(*satya*)-ness(*tā*))

sayam self control

sevā service, selfless service to God or man

sevak servant

shakti strength, power, ability, energy

shaktimān powerful

shānti peace

sharir body

sharirarup bodily (*sharir*) form (*rup*)

shāstra scripture, systemized knowledge

shāstri teacher, teacher of the scriptures

shāswat eternal

shishya disciple

shraddhā faith, reverent trust

shraddhāvān believer

shrāp curse

shuddh pure

sri auspicious word used at the beginning of a writing, honorific prefixed to names of gods, great men and celebrated works

swāmi Lord, master

swārpan self-offering

swarup image, form (lit. self(*swa*)-form(*rup*))

swatantra free

swatantratā freedom, independence, originality

tap austerity, penance, control of the senses, waiting for something for a long time
tāranhār savior
tarkashāstri philosopher, teacher of the *shastras* that refer to salvation
tatāstu amen

uddhār redemption, salvation, emancipation, deliverance
uddhārnār redeemer, emancipator, deliverer
uttam good, perfect

vāni voice, speech, language
vāsanā lust, inclination, impression on the mind of past actions which produce
   pleasure or pain
vibhuti dominion, riches, prosperity, divinity, ashes
vishuddhi purification
vishwās faith
vishwāsniya faithful
vishwāsu faithful

vishwāsyogya trustworthy
vivek discernment

yājak priest, official at a sacred sacrifice
yajña sacrifice, sacred fire sacrifice
yug age; four *yugs* make up the cycles of history in classical mythology; we are
    currently in the *kali yug*, or last and worst age

Preface

This book was first written in Gujarati in the mid 1950s.[1] This translation was produced as *Song of the Heart* (Sri Hriday Gitā) in 2014, and only some minor corrections have been made for this new printing under a new title. The translators have attempted to present a true presentation into English of the author's work, and to do so maintained numerous Gujarati (Sanskritic) words in the text. Numerous Sanskrit words are now accepted as part of an English vocabulary, like guru, yoga, karma and dharma (the latter spelled *yog*, *karm*, and *dharm* in this text, indicating their Gujarati pronunciations).[2] Many more rich terms from that Sanskritic world are welcomed into this text.

Which terms to so introduce, and when to simply translate into English, was a highly subjective process that the translators wrestled with. It will quickly be seen that no alternative words for "God" are introduced in this text. The reason for this is quite simple.

---

1. For more about the author and book see the appendix on page 180.
2. *Yog* or yoga appears mostly in chapter titles. This usage of the word is broader in meaning than what has become popular in English. The Bhagavad Gita uses yoga in each of its eighteen chapter titles, and Dhanjibhai is clearly alluding to that rubric in his own titles.

Dhanjibhai used only "*ishwar*" and "*parmeshwar*," neglecting numerous other rich Sanskritic terms that refer to the deity.[3] Seeing no importance in the alternative uses of these two closely related Sanskrit terms, we stayed with the English word "God" throughout the text. Similarly, "Lord" is used repeatedly throughout this book, always translating "*prabhu*." Yet here a few exceptions emerged, so where Dhanjibhai used "*swāmi*" instead of "*prabhu*" we indicate a meaning of "master."

At some points an active verb form in Gujarati is made passive in English in order to facilitate the adoption of Gujarati terms into the English text (i.e. *vishwās karvo* or "do faith/believe" in Gujarati becomes "have faith" in this translation). Plural Gujarati forms are also not indicated, just the singular root, and the English "s" is added at times, as has become conventional. We chose to simplify our transliterations of Gujarati words as this is not a text aimed at scholars; the distinction between long and short "a" is made throughout as this is quite fundamental. Rather than the pedantic ṛ for the seventh vowel, we transliterate with "ri" in accord with standard Gujarati transliteration.

---

3. The only exception is in 21.21 where he uses *dev* in referring to the weapons of God.

An English meaning is provided in the text for every Gujarati term so introduced, and a glossary at the end gives a complete list with some nuances of meaning. The standard Gujarati-English dictionary by P. G. Deshpande was used for the glossary. In sections of the text where a term is repeated, only the first use of the term is given an English definition.

Our thanks for the cooperation of the Gujarat Tract and Book Society in making this new English edition available.

The translators
November 2019